T0197150

NO MORE PRISONS

urban life
homeschooling
hip-hop leadership
the cool rich kids movement
a hitchhiker's guide to community organizing
. . . and why philanthropy is the greatest
art form of the 21st Century

BY WILLIAM UPSKI WIMSATT
author of *Bomb the Suburbs*

Soft Skull Press

Certain chapters of *No More Prisons* originally appeared in these publications:

"A Boof For People Who Don't Usually Read," "Bomb the Ghettoes," "Selling Bomb the Sub-
urbs in the Suburbs," "How Bomb the Suburbs Blew Up in My Face," "Triple Consciousness,"
"My Impossible Dream," and "Publishing Industry Motherfuckers" first appeared in *The
Chicago Reader*, 1996; "Hitchhiking as Sport" appeared in *On the Go*, 1995; "The Bet With
America," "The Most Feared Neighborhoods in America" and "What Bet? Which America?"
debuted in *In These Times*, 1995; Parts of "Schoolaholics Anonymous: How to Overcome
Your Addiction to School" first ran in the *New Haven Advocate*, 1997; "The University of
Planet Earth" came out in the *Dallas-Ft. Worth Met*; "Who's Afraid of Self-Education?" and
"The Black Homeschooling Movement" were in *XXL* in 1997; "19 Self-Schooling Strategies"
first revealed itself in *Utne Reader*, 1998; "The Basketball Kidnappings: How The Good People
of Hyde Park Are Sucking the Life Out of Urban Childhood" was born in *New City*, 1995; "A
City-Suburb Coalition? An Interview With Minnesota State Representative Myron Orfield,"
"Cities and Suburbs Unite! An Interview With David Rusk," and "A Wicked Civilization: An
Interview With James Howard Kunstler" originally found a home in *Tripod*, 1997; "Between
Prison and the Gated Community: How Our Fear of Crime Is Killing Us" was sprung upon the
world first in the vibrant and winsome *Adbusters*, 1997; "Who's Really Saving Our Cities? (It's
not who you think)" was originally printed in *Who Cares*, 1997; "The Detroit Millionaire
Who Couldn't Read: An Interview with John Payne" was first published in *Rappages*, 1998.

Wimsatt, William Upski.

No more prisons : urban life, homeschooling, hip-hop leadership, the cool rich kids
movement, a hitchhiker's guide to community organizing, and why philanthropy is
the greatest art form of the 21st century / by William Upski Wimsatt.
New York : Soft Skull Press, [c1999]
165 p. : ill. ; 22 cm.
Notes: Includes index.
Subjects: 1. Alternatives to imprisonment—United States.
2. Social action—United States. 3. Youth—United States—Social conditions.
4. Inner cities—United States. 5. Hip-hop. 6. Home schooling—United States. 7.
Community organization—United States. 8. Charity organization—United States.
HV9304 .W545 1999
364.4/045 21   2002276709

ISBN-10: 1-59376-205-4 ISBN-13: 978-1-59376-205-6

Soft Skull Press
www.softskull.com

Printed in the United States of America

TABLE OF CONTENTS

*To the young people of Chicago
and to young people around the world, we are depending
on you to appreciate and defend the gift of life.*

INTRODUCTIONS

ALL MY HATS AT ONCE

It isn't easy to write a real book—a book that's all that I am. I'm an artist daring to be original and I'm a journalist trying to be an honest man. But most of what's original is fiction, and most of what's true is old news. I'm a comedian and damn I be trippin', but I'm serious about what I say. I'm an entrepreneur trying to make money, but I'm a philanthropist giving it all away. I'm an organizer, fighting for everyone's fair share. But I'm also an environmentalist, and if everyone gets what we think is our fair share, there ain't gonna be shit but the flies. I have values I'm trying not to push on you, but I'm afraid that we're all going to die. So forgive me if I somehow offend you. My mother told me never to lie.

I'm pro-black but I laugh at racist jokes. I'm feminist but I'm a pig. I rarely tell people I'm a Jew. And I'm down with queers but if someone calls me "gay" I'll say, "Fuck you." And I'm a friend who'll be here for you. And you and you and you, now I'm spread thin. And I'm a person who loves unconditionally, but I have high-tech defenses the Pentagon couldn't get in. I'm blunt and I see through your bullshit, but I'm your cheerleader cheering you on. It's not easy to balance these hats on my head, they fall over my face like a dunce, but to me, that's what it means to be human, wearing all your hats at once.

And whether you like me or hate me, you can see what I'm saying is true. I'm giving you everything I have to give. Why shouldn't I expect the same from you?

Did you like that voice?
It sounds like something I would have written when I was 18.
Or 13.
I'm 25 now. And I still want 18-year-olds and 13-year-olds to read me.
But I've changed a lot in the past 7 to 12 years.
How about you?
A lot of people who remember me as a shit-talking graffiti writer may be disappointed with my evolution. I don't talk much about graffiti here. I'm more solution-oriented. And I don't talk as much shit. So if you're one of the people who liked how I was before, I hope you'll see that everything I'm doing now is a natural progression from what I was doing when I was 13 or 18 or 21.

When I was 13, I was break-dancing and doing graffiti and cutting school but unaware that I could quit. I was kicking it with people from the other side of the tracks, and interested in neighborhoods, but barely aware of urban planning, back room politics, or the legacy of historical change movements.

When I was 18, I was writing about hip-hop for magazines and newspapers. I took time off of college, but I didn't have a self-education plan. I read a lot about race, class, cities, social change, activism and community service. I got my first taste of the activist and do-gooder worlds. I was still barely aware of foundations or philanthropy.

When I was 21, I had published *Bomb the Suburbs*, a book on hip-hop, adventure, race, cities and social change. And I had a program: To put the money from the book into running a hip-hop community center, to find and publish young writers from the ghetto, and to hitchhike around the country trying to convince middle-class white people to overcome their "suburban mentality."

It was my greatest triumph and my greatest disappointment. Triumph because the book sold 23,000 copies which is unheard of for a self-published book on a shoestring budget. It was critically acclaimed, changed a lot of people's lives a little and a few people's lives a lot. A lot of people read it who don't usually read books.

Disappointment because it should have sold 230,000 copies but I knew nothing about book distribution or the basics of running a business. The community center died because we ran out of money and we weren't organized enough. It takes a lot more resources than we had to nurture and publish young writers from the ghetto. And it takes a lot more to change lives and institutions than speaking passionately, telling stories and asking tough questions.

So now that I'm 25, I'm studying all the powerful institutions and figuring out—in clever and ordinary ways—how to build institutions to seriously challenge them. That's how I went from running around the city to urban planning and politics. From writing on walls to real estate. From chillin' with cool kids in the ghetto to making appointments in suburban office parks with not-so-cool adults. From cutting class to the Self-Education Foundation. From helping broke friends to the Active Element Foundation. From hawking my book on the subway to "sales and marketing." From hand-me-down clothes to . . . now I own three suits. From breaking the law to studying the history of strategic social change. From denying my privilege as a well-to-do white person to taking responsibility for it.

I see my growth as a natural progression.

I want to help other young people in their evolution—from juvenile delinquency or prep school to public art and activism to becoming strategic, lifelong agents for creative historical change.

No More Prisons is a quick and dirty look at a handful of tiny emerging movements in five key areas that I'm excited about.

I'm sure there are many other areas that are at least as worthy: Campaign Finance Reform comes to mind. Fair wages, good unions. Boycotting sweatshops. Rainforest soil erosion. The extinction of endangered species. The mass torture of animals. The greenhouse effect and destruction of the ozone layer. The military-industrial complex, how it eats up our tax dollars and forces us to sell weapons to asshole dictators committing genocide against their own people. The mistreatment of women. Discrimination against disabled folks. Fear of queers. The brave new worlds of space, biotechnology, global capitalism . . . and other really important issues that I don't have any original insights about.

If one of these is your issue, I'm sorry.

I didn't have anything new to say about it.

I want to write about everything that matters and be all things to all people, but I can't. So I try to limit myself to writing from personal experience and creating combinations I haven't heard anyone say before.

That way I get to feel like I'm being original.

And you get to feel like you're reading a one-of-a-kind book.

The five areas I chose are just five areas I happen to know about from my limited experience on Earth. Five small glimmers of something bigger, five small windows of opportunity to act: Urban Life, because it reminds us of community and the race and class divides, and the history of fucked up social policy which makes it difficult for us to know and love each other. Homeschooling and Self-Education because we must all find our own educations, our own destinies, in a system that tells us we can't educate ourselves because it—the curriculum, the teacher, our parents—knows best. Hip-Hop Leadership because I grew up in hip-hop. It is my second family and I love it and hate it and know it needs leadership. The Cool Rich Kids movement not only for the obvious reason that you need cool people with money to do anything large scale, but also to symbolize how powerful all of us are. We are all rich kids. Most of the time, we do not comprehend how rich we are. A Hitchhikers Guide to Community Organizing symbolizes the marriage between fun and serious, adventure and commitment, the spontaneous and the strategic, doing for Self, and doing for the Whole. Why Philanthropy Is The Greatest Art form Of The Twenty First Century? Shit, it better be or the Twentieth might be the last century. Also, I want to reclaim the much abused word "philanthropy"—which means love of humanity—but you wouldn't know it by the narrow and ugly and deadening way most of it is done.

No More Prisons is a collection of snapshots swirling toward a synthesis. A lot of the stuff in here sounds young to me now. Many of the essays and interviews are four or five years old now. Everything in here is connected to everything else, but not all the connections are spelled out. Some you have to figure out for yourself.

I am an author who writes to my audience. The problem is, I have so many specific and separate audiences that to write for one is to alienate the rest. This book is where I get caught playing chameleon. For example, "The

Hitchhiker's Guide to Community Organizing is a synthesis of four versions of the same story written for four different audiences: One for a political magazine. One for a weekly newspaper. One for a literary magazine. One for a hip-hop graffiti magazine. The version printed here is a combination of all four.

Sound schizophrenic?

That's how I experience life in this segregated society.

Welcome to my life.

WHAT I WANT

I love it when you ask people,

"What do you *really* want?"

And they say,

"I don't know."

Yes, you do. You know what you want. You just think you can't have it. You feel like you want too many things and some of them are emotional and hard to put your finger on, or hard to put words to, and you're not sure how to get what you want. You might be afraid to be rejected. You might even be afraid that you'll get what you want. But deep down inside, you *know* what you want.

You know.

After we hadn't talked in at least a year, my friend Kie wrote me a letter and said she had spent a lot of the last year taking care of her mother who had cancer. She concluded her letter by saying that she had decided to become an astronaut because, "I know it's trite and obvious but you really do get only one life. If there's something you want to do and you're not doing it, you won't get another chance." She also said that she feels very close to me even though we haven't spoken in a year and that she will always love me no matter how sporadically we communicate. Also she said that she wasn't going to apologize for the letter (as she usually does) because "at this point in the relationship, I don't worry about being interesting."

I love Kie. I love the way she is.

Different phrases from her letter are still ringing in my head. Especially the one about *you really do get only one life.*

You really do get only one life. If there's something you want to do and you're not doing it, you won't get another chance.

Then she wrote, "This is a concept you've always had a good grasp on. You seem to go after the things you want."

I tried to think about myself and whether it was true. I think I feel most of the time like I'm a scared little puppy, afraid to open the doors too wide, taking certain leaps of faith, but usually not conscious of how *once in a life time* it all is. I thought, "What would I be doing if I really let all my fears go?"

My mind went blank.
I didn't feel like I had an answer.
All these thoughts flashed through my mind.
Climbing mountains.
Breathing.
Scuba diving.
Doing magic.
Walking through the jungle.
Driving a car.
Destroying all cars.
India, Thailand, Cambodia, Vietnam, Iraq, Jerusalem, Jordan, Egypt, Nigeria, The Congo.
Eating fruit.
Swimming in a river.
Being in prison.
Praying.
Making love.
Moscow, Italy, Sarajevo, The Philippines, New Zealand, Hawaii, Central America, Alaska, Siberia, Antarctica.
Telling people "Life is too short. I don't have time for that."
Jumping off cliffs.
Yelling like a dinosaur, "Rrrraaaaahhhhh!"
Living in a housing project in Chicago, the Robert Taylor Homes, Stateway Gardens, Cabrini Green, Rockwell Gardens or Henry Horner.
Singing my own music all the time. Ghostwriting songs on the radio.
Interviewing people I look up to.
Writing every morning, early before dawn, putting out a best-seller every year.
Making movies.
Helping start as many new and necessary organizations as Ralph Nader or Tracy Gary.
Serving on 50 to 100 boards of directors.
Having an organized work space so that I can take advantage of every opportunity.
Being part of a team of equals that do incredible things together.
Combining martial arts, break-dancing, ballet, tap, and gymnastics into my own dance form and doing it everywhere.
Telling everyone what I think of them.
The Pentagon, a gated golf community.

Owning my own home in the ghetto with no locks on the door, being part
of the community, painting every wall in the neighborhood with murals,
fixing up abandoned buildings. Turning lots into gardens.

Insisting on the best from everyone.

Helicopters, flares, head-spins, back-flips.

Hitchhiking and sailing around the world with a lap-top computer.

Not taking any shit.

Loving all children as my own.

Working my ass off, dripping with sweat, taking a shower.

Going to sleep dead tired and curled up in warm things.

Selling my favorite books to people everywhere I go.

Always carrying food for homeless people.

Not being afraid of anyone under any circumstances, even if they have a
gun in my face. Loving life so fully that I could penetrate any armor.

Carnival in Brazil.

Cuba. Puerto Rico. Haiti. Jamaica. Trinidad. Morocco. Japan. Mongolia.
East Timor. West Virginia. Madagascar.

Clipping every important article in magazines; keeping them on file for
instant consultation.

Having a huge family. Having every tenth person I see on the street be in
my family.

Being completely unfamous. Never be on TV or in the newspaper.

Laughing to myself whenever I like. Laughing at people wasting their lives
worrying why I'm laughing.

Finding the most amazing poor people in the world. Giving them money,
no strings attached.

Having hundreds of mentors I choose myself.

Fighting to the death.

Helping people who write better than me and who've lived more to publish
and distribute their own books, movies, and music.

Never being jealous of anyone.

Convincing cold, hardened rich people to live and love and use their privilege
to support people who could dramatically improve the course of history.

Maintaining my posture, my hearing, and my teeth.

Advise the president.

Keep everyone's secrets.

Live past 120.

Then start doing drugs.

Die alone on the streets of Chicago, penniless and laughing.

WHY ARE ALL YOUR FRIENDS IN PRISON?

Have you noticed more and more of your friends are in prison for seemingly minor charges?

Do you know why?

It's because the prison system has expanded four times since 1980.

Four times.

According to the U.S. Bureau of Justice Statistics, in 1980, there were fewer than half a million people in U.S. jails and prisons.

Now there are close to two million.

The violent crime rate has stayed about the same. In fact, it's 18% lower now than it was in 1980, according to the FBI's Unified Crime Report.

But four times as many people are in prison. Seven hundred new prisons have been built. The number of women in prison has skyrocketed from 12,000 in 1980 to more than 80,000 today—a seven-fold increase. Spending on law enforcement has increased by a factor of five.

In just 20 years.

The cycle goes like this: The media needs higher ratings to sell more advertising so they run more sensational crime shows that scare the public. The prison industry needs more people imprisoned to boost profits so they lobby for more prison construction. Politicians need to create jobs for construction workers and prison guards, and they need to be seen as tough on crime. They pass tougher crime laws and kill three birds with one stone: more low-skill jobs are created in the prison industry; campaign contributors in the prison industry are repaid; and the tough-on-crime image plays well with voters whipped into a false fren-

COMIC BY CHRIS SILVA AND VEVA SILVA

zy by the media over their fear of crime.

More than 60% of all prisoners now are incarcerated for non-violent

offenses—1.2 million people, according to the Bureau of Justice Statistics. A Senate subcommittee took a national survey of prison wardens. Now, these are prison wardens, not the most liberal of folks. The survey found that 92% of wardens believed "Greater use should be made of alternatives to incarceration." And more significantly, wardens believed that, "On average half the offenders under their supervision could be released without endangering public safety."

But prisons are a $100-billion-industry. A lot of money is being made. So the prisons must be built. The beds must be filled.

"It seems to me prisons need to be reserved for the most violent, most predatory members of society," says legendary Black Panther Eddie Ellis, who runs the Community Justice Center in Harlem. In 1997, he was named *Prison Life* magazine's 'Man of the Year.' "All these people who are drug addicts or who write bad checks, they don't belong in prison. The drug addicts are probably better dealt with in a public health setting because the socialization process in prison is very bad. A guy goes in for writing bad checks or for drugs,

and he comes out a hardened criminal with no options in life but to commit crime. And there's less and less positive or rehabilitative programs. I came out of prison after 25 years with a Master's in Theology and a B.A. in business administration from Marist College. Now all those programs have been cut. The most you can get is an eighth grade education. Who's going to make a better contribution to society? Me, or someone who's in there getting no higher than an eighth grade education? Who would you rather have living next to you?"

Thousands of laws have been passed since 1980. The Drug War was created. Gang laws enacted. Mandatory minimums and Truth in Sentencing laws took away judges' discretion in sentencing. Legal aid to poor people was cut dramatically. And a growing number of citizens (13% of all black men) are now ineligible to vote because of prior criminal records.

The ratio per capita of white to black drug users in the U.S. is roughly 1 to 1. But the sentencing rate of whites to blacks for drug possession is 1 to 10. The amount of crack you need to get a five-year mandatory minimum is 5 grams, but for powder cocaine it's 500 grams—which is interesting once you learn that 75% of those arrested for powder cocaine are white, and 90% of those arrested for crack are African-American.

Can you say "Systemic racism?"

Latinos are incarcerated at a comparable rate to blacks if you factor in INS (Immigration and Naturalization Service) detention facilities. Asian and Pacific Islander incarceration is small but fast growing. And Native Americans have the highest incarceration rate of any group—which is fucked up considering that they somehow managed to get along without any prisons for thousands of years before the rest of us got here.

Leave aside for a moment that police and judges aren't always fair. Leave aside that prisons break up families. Leave aside that prisons incubate disease,

not just AIDS, but TB, Hepatitis C and what will we hear about tomorrow? Leave aside that prison trains people to be criminals. Leave aside that they send people back out into the world with records that make it almost impossible to get any other job. Never mind what prison does to people mentally. Leave aside that the prison boom has forced dramatic budgets cuts for schools, colleges, after-school programs, drug rehab, job training, Head Start, affordable housing, legal aid—every social program that keeps poor people from being vacuumed into prison's terrible domain. (The annual cost of incarcerating a prisoner for one year is enough to put about seven people through community college or drug rehab.) Never mind that California has built 21 prisons since 1984 and only one university. Never mind that children as young

as 14 can be tried as adults and locked up with adults. Never mind the alarming growth of prison labor and prison privatization, which means that Wall Street is directly profiting from the prison industry. Never mind that the 13th Amendment outlaws slavery except in prison.

So it literally is slavery.

But never mind that, because if

we don't do something soon, it's about to get a lot worse. The Report of the National Criminal Justice Commission projected (in its excellent book *The Real War on Crime: The Report of the National Criminal Justice Commission* edited by Steven R. Donziger) that at the current level of growth, the prison population by 2020 will reach 12 million people. Approximately 63.3% of all black males age 18-34 would be incarcerated.

WHY WE LOVE PRISONS

One of the things missing from the conversation about prisons is why we are so attracted to them. From the time we are born we are put in a crib, seat-belted into a stroller, strapped into the back seat with childproof locks. We are driven in cars or buses to sit behind desks in classrooms. Our homes and stores and libraries have locks on the doors. Our schools have riot gates, security guards, video cameras, metal detectors. Our countryside is locked up with roads and highways. Our rivers and lakes are blocked and polluted. Even our parks have fences around them. Our feet need shoes. Fish belong in fish tanks. Animals are either pets in houses, specimens in zoos, dead on the side of the road or on plates. Workers work in factories, or cubicles or behind counters. Even our bosses must work in offices, the golden cages of the Market Age. Our experience of confinement is so much a necessity in our lives that we can scarcely imagine what it means to be free.

One of the aspects that's rarely mentioned about freedom is how profoundly frightened of it we are. Our spirits are so broken by modern life. We are so disheartened with ourselves and with others. We have been so hurt, we are reduced to the lowest common denominator: comfort, materialism, and a fear that is directed both outwardly (at the populations we build prisons for) and inwardly, in the sense of imprisonment we feel in our own lives and minds.

Almost everyone I have ever met is walking around with a cell block of imprisoned thoughts and feelings that they have rarely, if ever, allowed themselves to fully feel, much less express to another person.

We treat others the same way we treat ourselves. For every road and zoo and gated community and fence and lock and alarm system and prison we build, we are installing another prison cell in our hearts. We don't know our own minds for the same reason we don't know our own cities. There are too many bad neighborhoods, too many people inside of us who we don't want to see, too many bad feelings to let ourselves free.

I am as afraid as anyone else of violent crime. I've had my share of fantasies.

"What if we could just lock up all the bad people? Or what if we could just drop a bomb on them and kill them all at once?" I am not immune to these kinds of thoughts, even though I have been arrested several times and I am probably one of the ones who would be blown-up. (They always have to throw in a couple of mischievous white kids so it doesn't look like discrimination). Yes, inside of me too lurks a little Hitler who wants to get rid of all the people I don't like.

It is not bad to have bad thoughts. We all do. Most boys like to blow things up. And all of us have at least a little streak of cruelty. But then we have to investigate: "What are the real consequences to society of quadrupling the prison population every 20 years? Are there better ways to spend the $30,000 a year it takes to lock up each one of our nearly two million incarcerated fellow citizens? What is the effect of incarceration on families? What is the effect on inmates of being forced to adapt to prison life? How does it affect our society to socialize millions of non-violent offenders into violent prison culture? How does it effect people to watch their society adapt itself to the culture of the criminal justice system?

I've been feeling like I'm in prison myself lately. How do you work to change the system, and use the system's tools, without getting caught in the gears? I am crying now as I write this. I woke up this morning sick to my stomach and took a day off of work to come to the park and remember who I am. I have felt numb to life for months now. Only in the last few weeks have I begun to realize how burnt out I am, how much I have numbed myself to life. This may alarm people who know me. Everyone knows me as someone who enjoys life.

I had a conversation with a free person recently. It was almost too much to bear, like looking at the sun. I could feel a love for this person and also rage. Who is he to live free when I have so many masters? I caught a glimpse of how most people probably look at me. We are fascinated by freedom in movies and the freedom we project onto the rich and famous, artists, outlaws, indigenous peoples, children and others who are exempt from some or all of the rules the rest of us normally feel bound to. But in real life we fear freedom. It necessitates personal responsibility and self-trust.

I am a fan of personal responsibility and trust. It is the way they are defined in this society that I have a problem with. If you pave over nature, drive death machines called cars, and contribute to the greenhouse effect in this society you are considered responsible, normal, good. If you ride the bus, hitchhike, walk on the street in a poor neighborhood, or do not own a car, you are considered suspicious, if not an outright bum. If you downsize a company, pollute rivers and manipulate people into buying your products, you're just building your business career. If you sell weed to feed your family, you deserve to be imprisoned for five years.

Now I'm feeling bad for missing a day of work. I have an incredible job, a dream job, but still some days it feels like a prison. If I didn't take a day off work today I was gonna go crazy, or more likely I would just shut down, lower my expectations, and go that much more numb. I feel better now being in nature, speaking the truth.

What makes me mad is how alone I feel. How many other people get to feel as free as I am? I know I am one of the lucky ones. I have breathed the sweet air of freedom and I am not afraid of the way it fills my lungs. I was lucky to have two parents who loved me and gave me a nearly unblemished streak of good experiences. What impresses me is people who hold onto their faith and love, even though they have seen life's dark side. As damaged and alienated and sick as we are, maybe it's a miracle that even more of us don't live behind bars.

The rest of this book is not directly about prisons. If you want to learn more, please contact the following.

Prison Resources

- Center on Juvenile and Criminal Justice www.cjcj.org, 1622 Folsom St. San Francisco, CA. 94103 415-621-5661, 2208 Martin Luther King Jr. Ave. SE Washington D.C. 20020. 202-678-9282.
- Critical Resistance, 1212 Broadway #1400, Oakland, CA, 94609, 510-444-0484 (www.criticalresistance.org)
- Criminal Justice Consortium, 1515 Webster St., Oakland, CA, 94612, 510-836-6065
- Families Against Mandatory Minimum, 1612 K St. NW, Washington, D.C., 20006, 202-822-6700 (www.famm.org)
- Prison Legal News 2400 NW 80th St. #148 Seattle WA. 98117 www.prisonlegalnews.org
- The Shattered Lives Project (www.hr95.org)
- The Prison Moratorium Project (http://www.nomoreprisons.org)
- The Sentencing Project (http://www.sentencingproject.org/)
- Prison Activist Resource Center (http://www.prisonactivist.org/)
- California Prison Focus (www.prisons.org)
- The Stolen Lives Project (http://www.unstoppable.com/22/english/stolenlivesPROJECT/)
- Refuse and Resist 28 Vesey St. #2157, NY, NY, 10007, 212-766-1356 (http://www.calyx.com/~refuse/)
- Community Justice Center/Eddie Ellis, 103 E. 125th St., NY, NY, 10028 212-427-4545

A HITCHHIKER'S GUIDE TO COMMUNITY ORGANIZING

BY ERICA THORNTON

AREN'T YOU TIRED OF HAVING THE SAME
HAIRDO AS EVERY OTHER GHETTO BITCH?

Doesn't it bother you that every time you get your new weave in, with your fingerwaves and corn-rows, you come outside and every other bitch is sporting your do? **You'll never have to go through this again at Shaquanta's.** We specialize in making one-of-a-kind hair-weave creations for all Hoochies and Hoes.

Our specialties include the **C-Lo Special**. Tired of your man spending too much time shooting craps with his niggas and not with you? Our professionals have built the technology to **change your hair into the perfect area for craps**, including a backwall and even a place to store the dice. For fifty additional dollars we will add **secret compartments** so that five-o can't rush any of your games and take your nigga away.

Our pride and joy is **Shaquanta's Super Shop**. The shop, as we call it, is a **state-of-the art chamber** that cranks out one-of-a-kind do after one-of-a-kind do. We start out adding to your head **three-and-a-half feet of top-of-the-line weave**, then as you enter the chamber we run an electric current through your head to make it stand up in every direction. Following this, you enter the **wind tunnel** to give your hair shape, then we add glue and spackle to make sure it stays and has that **crusty feeling**. Finally, we give it a coat of Thompson's Water Seal to make it stand up to even the worst elements. To top all of that off, we will send any hairstyle through the **marvelous paint sprayer** so you can have all the **fly new colors no other hoe has**. So don't wait; run on down to Shaquanta's and turn yourself into a **Super Skeeza**.

A BOOK FOR PEOPLE
WHO DON'T USUALLY READ

"Tired of having the same hairdo as every other ghetto bitch?" didn't sound like an article you'd read in the newspaper. It sounded like something you'd hear on a rap tape, but none of us had ever *read* anything like it—so raw, so smart, written by a black Chicago public high-school student for an audience of his peers. (The author wished to remain anonymous so as not to shock the good people at his church).

Everyone felt the article was degrading, especially the black females present. The author and I tried to say that the world was degrading with or without this article. If we print it, maybe some people who listen to rap tapes will take off their headphones for a minute and start reading, an activity which could lead to *more reading, maybe even writing,* and less getting degraded by the world.

We fought about the article for two meetings straight. In the end, it came down to this: we knew of no other publication on the face of the Earth that would print it.

Ninety thousand publications were listed in the *Standard Periodical Directory* last year—and many more are unlisted. Is it too much to ask that there be at least one:
A) Written mainly by and for young people from the ghetto?
B) Not insulting to their intelligence?
C) Not boring?
D) Widely distributed?

We knew of no publication that fit these criteria. One of the goals of our paper *Subway and Elevated* was to come closer than anyone else. Most of the magazines we liked were too white and too whitely distributed. *Emerge* was too mature. Iceberg Slim wasn't mature enough. Hip-hop magazines come closest, but they're usually too starstruck and too shallow. Even the Internet, which has a Web site for *everything* doesn't have jack shit for inner-city youth (although there are a few exceptions, like http://streetlevel.iit.edu).

As usual, young people in the ghetto are canaries-in-the-coal-mine of a wider national problem. There has never been a genuine public life in America, let alone a public literature. Television talk shows are as close as we've come, but they fail the "not insulting to intelligence" test. No sooner were blacks allowed into American public life in the '60s than most whites abandoned it.

Middle-class blacks, as well as certain Latinos, Asians, church folks, artists, and poor whites played Human Buffer Zone. The window of time between the late '60s and the '80s is as close as America has come to being one nation. A study by Harvard Professor Gary Orfield showed that since the late '80s, public schools have been getting more segregated.

Mourning the decline of "public intellectuals" in America, Russell Jacoby wrote *The Last Intellectuals,* about a "broadly educated public." But does it include minorities, the young, or others who didn't attend elite colleges? Does it include people you see on the bus, at the community college or the public library? Does it include parents and students of public schools? Does it include people you'd see on State Street or any of the other truly public places in America? No offense to Jacoby, but his "broadly educated public" isn't the public at all. In a way, they're the anti-public. Scared of and sheltered from public life, most educated Americans have become silent partners of the automobile, highway and developer interests that have engineered public decline. In 1995 alone, 43% of federal funding for public transit was cut with bi-partisan support. Where was the "broadly educated public?" Driving their cars, reminiscing on how great a city Chicago used to be before they abandoned and decimated it. (Chicago has lost three-quarters of a million people since 1950.)

The concept of *Subway and Elevated* was to create a literature for what was left of the public. We were the only publication we knew of that was editorially free with no ads, no grants, and no fee. We wanted to tell sides of stories that hadn't been printed because they were either above or below the radar of acceptable journalism. The *Subway* side was for untold problems and dirt. *Elevated* was to show bright spots, strategies, and solutions.

The ultimate goal of *Subway and Elevated* was to revive public places in America—and call attention to their necessity—by placing works of beauty and value there that were impossible to obtain in stores. It was our little way of turning the tables on the reward structure in American life. If you drove a car, lived in the suburbs, and sent your kids to private school, then for once in your life you couldn't have one.

"The medium is the message," wrote Marshall McLuhan. Our message was in the distribution. We taped our paper to the train lines.

Four of us got arrested. That put a dent in our message. We needed a new message. A book! No one could arrest us for a book, we thought. Plus we could make money to pay for the paper, the lawyer and maybe a community center or two. According to *Books in Print,* more than 142,000 books were published in the U.S. in 1995. Guess how many addressed young people from the ghetto?

I wasn't from the ghetto but several of my friends were because I'm hip-hop. I had been interviewing hip-hop artists and passing out articles at hip-hop meetings every Sunday in the park. Already, there had been 20 books written on hip-hop, but outsiders wrote them all. *Gee, hip-hop really is an art form. These kids have a subculture and everything!* None of the books were by us. None of them spoke to our concerns.

Publishing people saw the word hip-hop in my cover letter and said no. Music books don't sell. We don't know who your audience is. Young people? Young males? Young *black* males? Maybe if you slip in some romance and market it to females you have a chance. But millions of people buy intelligent rap albums, I said.

One literary agent suggested I make a CD.

I had five other books partly written: hitchhiking and freight-hopping in the '90s, lies white people tell ourselves, youth politics and journalism, graffiti, cities vs. suburbs....Instead of writing five long boring books for five different audiences, why not write one short and sweet book forcing them all together?

I gathered $4,400, enough for 3,000 copies. (I called every printer in the phone book to find one cheap enough, and have money for 15,000 posters and glue to do every major artery in Chicago.

The editing process was the message. Most books have one editor. I begged 50 people to edit for me, including a 13 year old girl flunking eighth grade ("Cross out the boring parts" I told her). Then it had to pass The Subway Test. I read it aloud on subway platforms and demanded critiques from passing commuters—whereupon I really crossed out the boring parts. Now *that's* public literature, I said to myself. The New York Intellectuals of the 1950s and the New Black Intellectuals recently ordained by the *Atlantic Monthly* were cloistered snobs.

The title of the book, *Bomb the Suburbs,* appeared around Chicago. Frightened tourists took it literally. Kids assumed it was a rap group. Working people guessed it was a movie. Yuppies were under the impression it was avant-garde theater. A thousand people came to the book release party. "The largest integrated socio-political event I have witnessed in Chicago" according to one '60s activist in *Race Traitor.* People I barely knew slanged the book at high schools and junior colleges. It was the best-selling book almost everywhere in Chicago it was available: Literary Explosions, 57th Street Books, Booksellers Row, Tower, Afrocentric Pride, The A-Zone, UIC and DePaul, as well as mom-and-pop music and clothing stores where it was the only book. Most customers were young people age 14-25, it was reported to us. Most were male. Most were black. "It's the only book they come in here looking for on their own," Gail Hilliard, (manager of Kroch's and a Brentano's) told the *Chicago Sun-Times.*

To sell 1000 copies is considered success for a self-published book. Within three months we sold 3,000 with no distribution, no ISBN, no bar-code, and no listing in *Books in Print.*

NOT JUST A BOOK—IT'S A PLAN

That was fall 1994. By December, we printed a 10,000-copy second edition with a major new conclusion:

> "*Bomb the Suburbs* isn't just a book. It's also a plan. The plan is to do on a bigger scale everything we talk about in the book. For starters, we need a *Bomb the Suburbs* Building for the B-boy Homeless, a studio, computer lab, library, party space, kitchen, printing press and abandoned lots for gardens. Then we can publish and distribute other original books and albums at cheap prices; bring stability and creative alternatives to the city; serve as a national headquarters for the advancement of young people and the destruction of ghettos and suburbs; and keep a couple dozen of our friends from falling off the edge. If you like the book, let us know how you want to become part of The Plan."

I didn't have the luxury to wait for benefactors (they never came anyway). Some of my friends were already falling off the edge. Three of my more stable friends agreed to go in with me on a space. We looked for somewhere big and cheap on the south or west side. Nothing listed in the papers, not even the *Chicago Defender*. We settled for a giant basement called the "Vision Village." I wanted it re-named "The Suburbs" because it was in Wicker Park. So many people needed space so bad, they were constantly coming over, sometimes with bags of food, sometimes with no food for weeks at a time. Friends donated couches, a linoleum dance floor and books for a small library. We had exchange students from Brazil to Japan and dozens of activities, including a mini Chamber of Commerce for young entrepreneurs.

I was in charge of the writers' workshops. All narcissistic young writers fantasize they are part of a generation like the beatniks or the Harlem Renaissance who use the media and entertainment biz to engineer their own popularity. In my version, the group would be based not on what we wrote, but on *where* we wrote—not in cafes, bookstores or addresses on the World Wide Web, but in public places of the city. At our first reading, at the intersection of State and Van Buren downtown, about 40 people came. Passersby were stopping to listen. "What the hell are they doing?" One of the writers painted three-foot cardboard fish and hung them in nearby trees.

Our second reading at the 95th Street train station was not as successful.

Five of us were arrested on a string of goofy charges one of the officers invented. She had heard about *Bomb the Suburbs* and was under the impression that it instructed kids to go out and do graffiti. When we went to court, she tried to tell the judge that the five of us were "dancing and prancing," shoving books at elderly people who complained to them (anonymously of course).

BOMB THE GHETTOS

I was looking for a partner to take my place so I wouldn't have to be busy all the time. A friend I bailed out the previous year on gun charges beat his case and I had $1000 coming from Cook County Jail. I said damn, if I can risk $1000 bailing someone out for doing stupid shit, why can't I risk $1000 for something I believe in?

Somewhere in Chicago, I reasoned (oh so humbly, mirror, mirror on the wall) there was a writer more original, more broad-thinking, more ambitious, younger than I was, from the ghetto. If not, then there were five writers, one original, one broad-thinking, one ambitious, one young, one from the ghetto, and they could *collaborate*—mush themselves together into a Great Ghetto Writing and Publishing Messiah who would capitalize on the success of *Bomb the Suburbs* and create an inner-city kid publishing renaissance out of Chicago.

I brought the idea to the writers group and we decided to throw a festival, a summer-long workshop series, and a contest at the end of the summer. It was called, "Bomb the Ghettos—Too many ghettos in writing, not enough writers in the ghetto."

We invited, "Rappers, journalists, comedians, graffiti writers, critics, cartoonists, poets, playwrights, griots, novelists, and shit-talkers"—with no separation between categories. The best rappers and novelists *are* journalists. The best critics *are* comedians *and* playwrights *and* poets. Poetry and graffiti aren't categories of writing, they're tools. The only worthwhile category of writing is *great* writing, the more tools you use the better.

According to our guidelines, contestants could enter, "A series of ten lyrical-video-graffiti-journalistic-Ph.D.-screenplay-CD-novels. One extraordinary sentence on a folded-up napkin—or in 20 foot letters hanging off the Sears Tower!...The format is entirely up to you, but don't think you're going to win just by doing what you already do. You have to grow. You have to push yourself."

Emphasis was placed on, "How cleverly you get your words to people who wouldn't ordinarily read or listen to them. Teaming up is encouraged! (Photos, tapes, or press clippings of the work(s) are fine, but keep in mind, it's your words and how you *hustle* them that matters . . .)"

No one had ever heard of anything like it. Within two weeks, various publishing people donated second, third and fourth prizes totaling $800. Everyone was excited. We had a movement to be part of. We blanketed downtown with giant green posters. Taped them on half the train cars on the two main lines. Sent them to every neighborhood library and every high-school English department. Talked it up on hip-hop radio and at poetry readings, as well as mainstream media outlets. There was also graffiti. I have no idea how it got there.

We expected at least 3000 people to come and spark off a revolution in the world of publishing. But revolutions cost money and I had virtually stopped selling books. By April, I had 9,000 *Bomb the Suburbs* and no money. Artists were asking for royalties and the Chicago market was drying up. I needed to go on tour but I was a city kid and I didn't know how to drive. One month until summer, I began writing a press release, not only to publicize what I was doing, but to figure it out.

THE BET WITH AMERICA

To sell the book in other cities, I would hitchhike and walk through neighborhoods most white Americans don't even like to drive through. I didn't have a sound-bite message. My real message was a little too complicated to say. It was expressed not in the book, but through the book, by the structure and process of creating it.

"I want to make a bet with America," I began to write. "I'm betting my life."

I believe America is becoming a nation based on fear—not only of crime and so-called bad neighborhoods, but of strangers in general—and it's destroying everything that's good about us: Our democracy, our diversity, our freedom.

The good news and bad news is (this I will bet you), America isn't even that scary yet. To convince you of this, I'm hitchhiking across America and going to all of the so-called bad neighborhoods including the neighborhoods in your town you're the most afraid of.

If I get killed, I lose the bet.

If I win the bet, you have to consider what I say.

I believe that running away from the people we fear most—what I call the suburban mentality—is the source of our deepest problems in America, from violence and drugs to the economy to the mediocrity of our public life (politics, media, schools, architecture and public transit).

I'll be coming to your town soon to visit your most feared neighborhoods, and to talk about my new book *Bomb the Suburbs,* which discusses creative ways to overcome the suburban mentality in all of us. Please come see me when I'm in town (if I haven't already lost the bet) and tell me your ideas.

Because as Americans, we have a choice to make about fear. Either we begin facing the people we fear now and treating them as we'd want to be treated, or 10 and 20 years from now, we're really going to have something to fear. I'm betting my life to convince you of this.

The medium of travel was the message. My walk and my talk were the same thing.

I printed 5000 "Bet With America" posters. My parents confiscated almost all of them. "We're not worried about the ghettos," they said (lie), "we're worried about some crazy like the Unabomber taking this as a dare."

I decided to accept rides from all crazies and hang around all ghettos as late at night as possible.

If Newt Gingrich's "Contract with America" was putting America's butt on the line for a cynical suburban future, I was going to put mine on the line for a hopeful urban one. Newt Gingrich's book tour included 21 stops, so I was gonna do 27. I left with $50, a book bag, and nowhere to appear in most cities. A 15-year-old girl named Amanda Klonsky saved me. She volunteered as tour manager, taught herself the job, arranged publicity and refused to be paid. Aren't there child labor laws against that?

HITCHHIKING AS SPORT

The reason I don't get drunk or smoke herb anymore is the same reason I don't watch horror movies or play phony-ass video games or write my name on anything I didn't create. Drug highs are dull to me. Horror movies fuck with me when I'm alone at night. I usually have better things to write than my name, and the only video game that holds my attention is the video game of life.

Passive pleasures aren't for the young. When I'm old and dying, that's when I'm gonna do my drugs and watch my scary movies. The next time they catch me writing *upski upski upski* on something, I'm gonna be a senile motherfucker in a wheelchair. But not while I have a mind. Not while I have a body.

I love hitchhiking as much as I love bombing, but for opposite reasons. Bombing, you avoid people and light. Hitchhiking, people and light are all you've got. Bombing assumes society is fucked up. It can't be reasoned with. It has to be bombed. Hitchhiking assumes there are still good people left and you have to meet them. Bombing, you're telling everyone who you are.

Hitchhiking, you're learning about others.

And you always meet the coolest fucking people when you hitchhike. They're all independent thinkers. Many either work for themselves or own their own businesses. Many are gay or religious, but few will attempt to convert you. Many are ex-cons but few will attempt to fuck with you. Active criminals are usually too paranoid to pick you up. (Bushwick Bill, you watchin' too much TV).

The problem with hitchhiking is that there are no books written about it that are up to date. A lot of people who used to hitchhike in the '60s and '70s say they'd never do it today. *American Pictures* author Jacob Holt, probably the greatest hitchhiking writer of all time, isn't really around much anymore.

Sorry them. The people who pick me up today are like a Who's Who of the most extraordinary people in America. I'd like to write a feature story on every last one of them. I've hitchhiked a total of about five months now, been all over this country in hundreds of cars. Never once has a real sicko picked me up. A couple of guys trying to put their hands on my leg. That's about it.

I would say one out of every 50 American drivers, given the right circumstances, will stop for a hitchhiker. On average, it takes me 20 to 25 minutes to get a ride. The qualities that make each of them willing to pick me up—a combination of generosity, independent-mindedness and willingness to risk—appear to reflect the way they act in other areas of life.

I had imagined before I hitchhiked that mainly the people who'd pick me up would be truckers and carloads of burly guys with tinted windows and menacing mustaches. Wrong. Truckers almost never pick me up because of the liability (one in 100 rides), and you almost never get picked up by groups of people (one in 40). Tinted windows never pick you up because they're too fucking cool, and groups rarely pick you up because they don't need anyone to talk to.

Females by themselves (one in 10 rides) pick me up more often than couples (one in 50). But once I went to Wyoming and back with Gin Kilgore, a white woman, and most of our rides were from couples and truck drivers! Blacks pick me up about one in 40. Both ex-convicts (one in 10) and self-made millionaires (one in 50) tend to pick me up in numbers greater than their share of the population. In Camden, New Jersey, I got a ride from a black, ex-convict, self-made millionaire in a Jaguar whose own brother had just been murdered two months earlier by a stranger.

And now he's picking up a white boy at the side of the road because "You looked like you needed a ride." This is what I mean about character. Of all the people who've picked me up so far, I'd say less than one-fifth identified themselves as leftists. Some of the people I got along best with were racists, rednecks, conservatives and evangelical Christians. Anyone who picks up hitchhikers in this day and age gets a gold star in my book.

THE VALUE OF A GHETTO EDUCATION

I'm kinda hoping I'll get my ass whupped on this trip. It hasn't gotten whupped in a long time, and I'm a guy from a comfortable background, so not only would I deserve it, but a decent ass-whuppin'—much as I'd hate it at the time—would probably do me some good.

But that's not why I'm hitchhiking around America this summer or walking around the most feared neighborhoods in each city, two activities I have been told are going to get me a whupped ass or worse.

Most people, when they find out I'm doing this, don't know how to process the information.

What's the catch, they want to know. Are you packing a gun? Do you run into the neighborhoods and then run back out? Do you walk around in the morning with a hood over your head so nobody sees you except for people going to work? No, no and no. What's the catch? The catch is that if you're a white male in America but don't act like an asshole, have some wits about you, and treat others as you'd have them treat you, it is not particularly dangerous to walk around by yourself, in any neighborhood in America at any hour of the night or day. The catch is that most white guys in America think these neighborhoods are dangerous because most white guys in America don't know how to treat people. (With white women the issues are somewhat different, but if anything a lot more white women live in the ghetto than white men do.)

But so what if some white guy can walk around in the ghetto! What the fuck good does that do? What's the fucking point? That's not organizing against racism. That's not struggling for social justice.

Really? Well how do you even begin to organize against racism or fight against social injustice when most of the white and middle-class people who are supposedly against racism are afraid to set foot in the very neighborhoods where the most oppressed people live? And when an entire generation of young people are being classified as criminals?

So yes, I think that has something to do with fear. It's true, me walking around the ghetto doesn't directly change anything other than my own understanding of the world. I hope that it will make people who read about it question their own fears which fuel the building of more prisons and gated communities, slamming the window on the fingers of opportunity.

THE MOST FEARED NEIGHBORHOODS IN AMERICA

So far this trip, I've been to Cleveland, Pittsburgh, D.C., Baltimore, Philly, New York and Boston. I accept rides from anyone who stops and I never ask to get out of the car unless I have to go to the bathroom. Every city I get to, I wander around for at least eight hours, usually more, and spend at least half of that time in neighborhoods that people tell me are bad.

I went to East Cleveland at sunset, the Southeast Side of Cleveland after dark.

I walked up North Avenue in Baltimore at midnight on a Saturday Night, down Pennsylvania Avenue at 2 AM. The next afternoon, I walked through Middle East.

In Pittsburgh. I started in these projects in the North Hills around midnight: Federal Street at 1 AM, the Hill District at 2 AM and Homewood the next afternoon. These three black people who I asked directions from told me not to go to Homewood. They said, "Why do you want to go to Homewood? Here, we'll give you money. Take a bus."

I said, "Have you ever heard of John Edgar Wideman? He's one of my favorite writers and he writes about Homewood."

They said, "Yeah, but you don't want to go there unless you have a gun."

"A gun?" I said, "I don't even have mace."

"Please! Let us give you money for a bus."

Please! Homewood is a nice, peaceful, workingclass neighborhood. There is one high-rise project. It looks like a luxury condominium.

The next day it was Florida Avenue in the Shaw district of Northwest D.C. at dusk, Northeast at night, Southeast and all over Anacostia. Anacostia is supposed to be the most fucked-up area. I walked around for like two hours among modest homes with neat lawns. Finally I came to a school yard with all these guys hanging out on the corner. Someone had written "WAR ZONE" on an electric box. I went over and asked the guys for directions. The only place I encountered any hostility was right on the border between DuPont Circle, a white area, and Shaw an historic black neighborhood near Howard University. I was putting up a poster that said "Bomb the Suburbs" on an abandoned building. A Howard student shouted, "We're gonna bomb your ass," from the window of his passing jeep. He kept driving.

West Philly up Market Street at night, then all in and around North Philly, Richard Allen Homes, the Latino section around 5th, 3rd, 7th to Erie St. then zig-zagging back through the black part from 11th to 23rd. And those projects just South of South Street. Philly was the only city that really scared me. In one long, hot North Philly afternoon, I got dunked in fire hydrant sprinklers three times.

New York City was surprisingly nice. The South Bronx I walked around for four hours, before and after sunset. Mill Brooks Projects, the Mitchell Homes, and about four others, all of them were totally integrated, well-taken care of, and bustling with life. Those stretches of war-torn buildings they show in all the movies covered a very small area and most have since been torn down. No one offered to sell me drugs, and only one wino asked me for spare change. Harlem at night, Alphabet City in the morning, and a huge zig zag through Brooklyn: East New York, five or six projects in Brownsville, then Crown Heights, East Flatbush, Bed-Stuy. I was like, "Where are all the bad neighborhoods?"

Boston barely even has a ghetto. I walked all through all the projects in Mission Hill, Roxbury and Dorchester on the 4th of July from sunset 'til 1Am. The worst that happened to me was one guy throwing a fire-cracker at me out of a car, and these giggling 10-year-old girls, throwing water down on people through their screen window overlooking Blue Hill Avenue.

What business do I have in these neighborhoods? It's a crucial part of my education. It lets me see first-hand that my parents and teachers and everyone else I have been listening to all my life don't necessarily know what the fuck they're talking about.

I've got about 14 more cities left to go. Every neighborhood I go to, I head straight for the public housing, walk through the courts, cut across abandoned lots, or head down whatever streets or alleys seemed the scariest to me. Conventional wisdom about crime says I should have been killed ten times over. But nothing has ever happened. The only crime that's happened to me so far is a white girl from Monroeville, a suburb of Pittsburgh, stole my diary and some jeans out of my bag as souvenirs.

I'm not trying to say slum neighborhoods are safe. Especially if you live there and are related to the drug trade, or if you act either phony, or nervous or condescending, or talk shit, or if you're walking around with an expensive video camera.

Then again, if you do any of those things, you probably need to get your ass whupped—part of your education in this ass-whuppin world.

WHAT BET? WHICH AMERICA?

I "bet my life" I could hitchhike across America and walk through the "most feared neighborhoods" without anything happening to me. I almost won the bet. I almost proved my fellow white Americans are paranoid and irrational. Unfortunately, I failed. As two newspapers have now revealed, I am a fraud.

After dutifully sleeping on sidewalks in North Philly and a cemetery in Detroit, trying unsuccessfully to run a publishing business from pay phones, and going out of my way to walk through the projects in the middle of the night, I began to feel silly. The point of my tour was to spark readers to examine their fears of the ghetto, of black people, of Latinos, of strangers, and of public life in general (what's left of it).

Some thought my tour had a different point. One time I was selling the book in Lower Manhattan and this businessman approached me from across the sidewalk:

"Hey, is that serious?"

No, it's a metaphor.

(It didn't seem like he heard me.)

I asked him why he was interested.

"I hate the suburbs too. Listen, do you have a card or something with an address on it?" I gave him my packet.

As soon as he got it in his hands, he was like a-ha.

"I'm gonna send this to the FBI, and to Newt Gingrich and you're gonna be the poster child for the 1996 Republican convention—you schmuck!"

He walked away.

I need to start carrying a tape recorder!

It would be the perfect Republican wedge issue. Bob Dole against a book. Or Bill Clinton could use it. It could be this year's Sister Souljah—even better because he wouldn't lose black votes to Colin Powell.

As my friend Gin told me, "Bet with America? Ha! I'd be willing to bet my life against America." No Gin, people like you and me need to put some ass on the line. We have no right to be cynical. That's what I would like to have told her. But now I have been exposed. Two weekly newspapers—*Everybody's News* (Cincinnati) and *City Pages* (Minneapolis)—have pointed out that I didn't visit their "most feared neighborhoods." In essence, I cheated on my bet.

Why did I cheat?

I cheated because America cheated. How can I make a bet with America when America never took me up on the bet? By the time I got to Cincinnati and Minneapolis, I was really tired and I was like look, I'm not afraid of these little neighborhoods. I can't even pretend to be. I was feeling like a ridiculous toy, a white would-be hero making a big deal out of walking through neighborhoods millions of people live in every day.

People were focusing on me instead of applying the bet to their own lives. My mom, for example was terrified of hitchhiking. Even in the '60s, she didn't hitchhike. I convinced her to hitchhike with me to Cincinnati and Columbus, Ohio. It was super easy and we had a great time. Did she change her views of hitchhiking? No. She's still just as terrified.

A few people seemed inspired and I didn't want to let them down. I went back to the bet again. It was easy, ordinary, just another chore. I was sleeping on the sidewalks of East Oakland and South Central L.A. with $500 in my pocket, standing along highways like, "Could one of you serial killers please pick me up? I have a 7 PM book reading to get to." It wasn't that I overcame my fear—it was crowded out by evidence.

Easy for you to say! You're not black. You're not a woman.

I don't know what to say to women. I know what to say to men about raping women, but what can I say to women? I know a Colombian girl Linda, from Jackson Heights, Queens, who ran away from home and hitchhiked to California when she was 16, no problem. I also met a black woman from D.C. who almost got raped and killed hitchhiking to New York. And I recently heard about another woman, a friend of a friend, who was killed hitchhiking from Nevada to California.

My friend Matt and I hitchhiked to Minneapolis. Matt is a "brotha" although I guess he's a "fine brotha" because we got more than the usual ratio of rides from women, including Karen Van Meenen, an editor at *Afterimage* film magazine. Two other women with their children pulled over to give us a ride. And a petite medical technician from mainland China picked us up in a luxury car.

She seemed at ease.

"Aren't you afraid to pick up strangers? Don't you watch American TV?" I asked her.

"You can't live like that," she said.

I thought of all the tough guys who wouldn't let us hop in the back of their pickup trucks.

At a book reading in San Francisco, I was challenged "not to go" to Hunter's Point (the largest black neighborhood in the city). A tough white guy named Mike (former graffiti writer in training to be a cop) offered to give me a tour of San Francisco, then drop me off in Hunter's Point. "Just don't go to Sunnydale," he added.

Sunnydale?

"Don't go there," emphasized a black woman. "It's really not worth it.

You won't be able to do anybody any good if you get killed. The ghetto in San Francisco is not like on the East Coast. Black people here are so isolated. So in a way they're even angrier."

Everyone has a reason why their black people are the scariest.

"Who wants to come with me?" I asked.

It was Saturday night. A bunch of people standing around. No one said anything.

"I'll come," said a small well-dressed young woman. She hadn't spoken all night. Everyone glanced at her nonchalantly and then quickly looked away. Even her friends didn't say anything to her.

Her name was Lisa Mir—from Newton, MA, a student at Pomona College. She had never been to a ghetto before. Mike drove us to the far end of Sunnydale. It was midnight. He tried to convince us not to get out of the car. Lisa and I walked in circles until 4 AM through Sunnydale, Hunter's Point, and a couple of housing projects on the way back to the Mission district.

"Get the fuck out of here!" someone shouted from a slow moving van. We were on a dark side street. Lisa didn't flinch.

After a summer of interviews and bookstore appearances, Lisa went the furthest I've seen anyone go in curbing their ghetto-avoidance pattern, among the least talked about gaps in American life. Which reminds me of an analogous gap in our literature. We need a literature about being spoiled. Enough of this literature about struggle! Most people who read in this country are spoiled and boring, yet all they want to read about is struggle and adventure.

The only white people I know who realize it's safe to live in the ghetto are the ones who've actually lived there. A few other whites tell me that I'm wrong, naive, lucky, lying or crazy. A least they're up-front about it.

Most whites I meet are neither experienced, nor up-front. They tell me they agree with me, or they admire me, or they change their attitudes, or they change the subject. But how many so far have changed their address?

Why should they? Everyone I meet or know well brings out a different part of my personality. My mother brings out one side. My father brings out another. The more kinds of people I know or know well, the more sides of my personality get developed. Any people I don't know or don't know on their own terms, not only do I not know them, I don't even know that part of myself. Most people I meet are walking around with less than half of a personality, clutching desperately to what little they have.

People with underdeveloped personalities aren't really in a position to make informed choices in their personal lives, let alone figure out how to organize against racism, or struggle for social justice. I don't care how long you've been reading *In These Times* or how astute you are when you're talking to your like-minded buddies. Without friendship among all the different kinds of people who are unhappy with the current system, then progressive organizing is impossible and progressive principles are empty. Social justice grows out of your social circle.

People in slums are not the only ones who I need to have in my social circle and they're not the only ones who deepen my personality. They're the most immediate, the most difficult, the most terrifyingly direct (next to women, that is). One day, I will marry a woman, and one day I will move to the ghetto. Both of these things will make me into a much better person than I am now. Not because marriage or an address means anything in and of itself. Especially if you are a bad neighbor or a bad spouse. It's the community and the love that counts.

In the meantime, I count on my close female friends and friends from the ghetto to constantly remind me how spoiled I am, how sheltered I am, how off is my sense of proportion, how selfish are my instincts, how dull is my character, how weak and how cowardly I am. These are the routine lessons that I need to constantly learn. Occasionally, there is a really unexpected one.

A few months ago, I was on the phone with a rapper I met named Rhyme Fest. Fest is 17, a dropout from South Shore, not one of Chicago's better public high schools. We were arguing about the politics of me dating a "sista." Finally, I said, "Well Fest, let's pretend you were me. What would you do?"

Fest thought about it for a while. "Don't get offended, dog. But I'm gonna tell you honestly."

"Be straight-up," I said.

"I think you need to read more books, dog. Because . . . you can tell that you have a lot of good ideas, but if you'd read more books it would help you express yourself more articulately."

SELLING 'BOMB THE SUBURBS' IN THE SUBURBS

I won't bore you any more with my adventures on the road. I'm going to bore you with the same thing that bored me: the drudgery of selling a book.

The whole summer was a blur of posters, glue, hitchhiking, walking through the projects, running the business by pay phone, sleeping, eating if I was lucky, washing up and showing up to the next reading. It wasn't how most authors spend their summer tour.

If the reading hadn't been publicized, I'd walk around the neighborhood hustling the book, flirting to get people to come. Half a dozen drag queens showed up to my reading at the Eye of Horus in Pittsburgh. Someone else came because they thought "free reading" meant free Tarot card reading.

During the tour, I sold fewer books in bookstores than on the street. I love to see people's faces the moment they register the book. Some of them laugh involuntarily. Others look away or do things with their eyebrows. The hipper that people looked—the more sunglasses, headphones, body piercings and tattoos they adorned themselves with—the less curiosity they displayed. Nearly everyone who took an interest in *Bomb the Suburbs* wore unassuming clothes.

"I'm *from* the suburbs," was a common remark.

"Do they read out there?"

The most common question, "What's the book about?"

I got tired of answering this question. I felt like, Please! What is your life about? It's about a lot of things. It's complicated. It's a book about white people. White people and bombing. Timothy McVeigh wrote it from his jail cell in Oklahoma when he changed his mind about the federal building.

I got tired of answering questions. I got tired of always talking about the book and never having time to read other people's books.

Hey, what's that book about?

It's about seven dollars.

Or "six" or "five" or "four" or "here" depending how broke they looked.

Seattle was the worst. So phony. One of the richest cities in the world and nobody has any money. (Why are they downtown shopping?). I poured the books onto the sidewalk and people just stepped on them. The only person who bought a book was a black man in a wheel chair who insisted I take his last four dollars.

I convinced my friend Matt that we should bring our dog Foxy with us to Minneapolis, Madison and Milwaukee. We almost skipped Milwaukee—there was nowhere to read. At the last minute, someone got us a café. When we arrived, I saw a cluster of young people standing outside. I went over and tried to sell them the book. They looked bewildered.

"Haven't you seen the paper? *The Shepherd Express* did a cover story on you. We all came here to see you . . . and . . . *that's the mayor."* They pointed behind me.

"Hi, I'm Mayor Norquist. This is my wife Susan. We want to buy a copy of your book." I'd been quoted as saying "If I were Mayor, I could eliminate graffiti in 15 minutes." A hundred and fifty people came. Everyone thought I was famous. The Mayor seemed a little disappointed when he found out that my method of eliminating graffiti involved turning all of the public surfaces that are illegal to write on into "legal walls" and hiring graffiti writers to paint public murals with neighborhood kids and maintaining them.

Three hours was the minimum length of a *Bomb the Suburbs* reading. Not because I'm a good talker; most people who go to hear an author talk really want to hear themselves. All I had to do was ask the questions. Audiences loved this. In Minneapolis, we went eight hours. "White people therapy sessions" Matt called them.

To Matt I say, "Fuck what you black people think. The white man got to have Knowledge of Self! That's the first level of the pyramid!"

Worried sick I might run out of water in the desert, my parents convinced me to fly home from L.A.. They paid for the ticket. I felt spoiled. Newt Gingrich had beat me—I only ended up doing 19 cities.

Bomb the Suburbs received no acknowledgment from major magazines, newspapers, library or publishing trade magazines. I almost got booted from the ABA (American Booksellers Association) convention for hawking the book without a booth. Toward the end of the tour, a producer from *Prime Time Live* called and said he wanted to collaborate with me on a hitchhiking series. Here it finally was, my 15 minutes of fame. I meditated carefully on how to use it for some greater good. He canceled the show and decided to do his own show hitchhiking across the country.

People were calling me, "Turn on Channel 7. Turn on Channel 7. This guy's doing your story."

When I saw the way he treated it, I felt lucky he left me out.

PUBLISHING INDUSTRY MOTHERFUCKERS

The first 13,000 copies were almost gone but I hadn't made any money. One of the themes of Bomb the Suburbs is how to have equal friendships with people unequal to you on the socioeconomic ladder. The 42 biggest contributors and editors got their royalties before I broke even. The royalty structure was the message.

Some people I dealt with had a different message. Our biggest distributor, Inland, filed for Chapter 11 financial reorganization/bankruptcy and fucked us for what would have been our first $6000 profit. Kroch's and Brentano's, our biggest Chicago account, melted-down over the summer, liquidating our assets. Hundreds of books went unaccounted for at every step of the process.

I don't regret chances I've taken with independent bookstores. Without them, small press books like *Bomb the Suburbs* wouldn't exist. You need local sales to establish a record for distributors. Supporting independent bookstores becomes a matter of free speech.

When was the last time you read a book criticizing Barnes & Noble, Borders, Crown, Waterstones, Ingram, or Baker & Taylor? Even *The Baffler* hasn't. The most direct criticism I've seen appeared not in the alternative press but in the untouchable *New York Times*. It reported major publishers pay chains in the millions to get their books displayed at the front of the store. How disgusting. I thought they put *Bomb the Suburbs* in the back as a matter of *taste*. Angry? Who me? No, I'm just a small business. I'm *friendly*. Nice chain bookstores. *Thank* you for carrying my book!

After traveling the country, watching independent bookstores struggle and go out of business, I feel lucky to live in a city where there are independent bookstores left. Small bookstore people I talk to anticipate the next three years will be especially hard because superstores are over-extending themselves fighting for market share. Eventually, many superstores will be forced to scale back selections, close branches, raise prices, or go bankrupt. Until then, independent bookstore people are praying for customer loyalty.

Considering our lack of distribution and publicity outside Chicago—and considering my terrible business sense—the book did surprisingly well. Independent bookstores like St. Mark's in New York and Midnight Special in L.A. sold more than 200 copies each. A manager at The Bookstore on West 25th Street in Cleveland told me it was their best-selling book ever, except for maybe *The Autobiography of Malcolm X*. It stayed on the Tower Top 40 for three months and was Tower's #1 best-selling book internationally for a week—with no traditional publicity.

At least a dozen college courses (in more than five different departments!) added it to their curriculum. I got more than 1000 letters. Renown critic Salim Muwakkil chose it as one of his top five books of the year. *Utne Reader* picked me as their youngest person to be an "Utne Visionary." Carl Upchurch, organizer of the National Gang Peace Summit called it, "the best $7 you'll ever spend" and out of the blue an 18-year-old waitress from Seattle named Kristin Brown sent me $40 to "keep writing."

As far as the publishing industry was concerned, I began to wonder. How many more posters must I plaster up, how many more asses must I pucker up, and who exactly do I have to sleep with (silicone? dentures?), before I can be considered a publishable author?

And what about writers who don't have $4,400, aren't egomaniacs and write better than I do? Most will never be published because motherfuckers in the publishing industry—whose job it is to find and nurture these writers—are too cloistered to do a competent job.

But would their next manuscript pass The Subway Test?

HOW 'BOMB THE SUBURBS' BLEW UP IN MY FACE

To see where I went wrong with Bomb the Suburbs, you have to go back to the beginning and ask me why I started writing in the first place. It wasn't for the noblest of reasons.

I started writing for the same reason I started doing graffiti and politics. I was an awkward 11-year-old, trying to fit in, never quite succeeding. I would come home from school frustrated. I would hide in the school library during lunch hour so nobody would see I had no one to eat lunch with—so no one would see I didn't have any friends. My graffiti, articles, and leaflets were my classified ads to the world. I wanted people to like me. Norman Mailer's *Advertisements for Myself* may as well be the title of everything I ever wrote.

I wanted to remove the barriers that were preventing people from liking me. I wanted to get rid of ghettos and suburbs. I wanted the kids who read books to do graffiti and the kids who did graffiti to read books. Past age 11, almost every friend I made I made through writing of one kind or the other. The more people began to like my writing, the more I began to like myself. If I wrote a whole book, imagine how many personal problems it would solve!

My personal problems? They're the same as everyone's. Feeling insecure and inferior makes me judgmental, arrogant, competitive. Feeling ignorant, I try to become knowledgeable, smart, experienced. Feeling puny in the hugeness of the world, I crave respect, power, strength. Feeling spoiled and sheltered, I grasp for excitement and risk. Feeling lack of love, I break hearts and flee closeness. Desiring freedom, I put myself in situations where I can't have much of it. Needing to feel good and innocent, I disguise my ugly side and manipulate people with niceness.

Needing things, and hating myself for needing them, I simultaneously run toward and away from my needs. I concoct substitutes to feed myself emotionally without having to admit I am hungry. That's how I came up with the idea to get people to like me by writing a book.

But a substitute is a substitute is a substitute. Somehow I could not get around that. Neither talent, money, popularity nor sex could free me from my emotional longings to see things as they are, to see myself as I am, to love myself as I am, to do what I'm capable of, and to share my love with the universe.

The more I tried to sneak past my needs, the more they caught up with me. I remember looking for role models, someone to show me a better way, but everyone I looked to was either a hypocrite, ineffective, or out of touch.

All my life, I felt that as much as I tried to get things right, a lot of life's basic lessons eluded me. I felt certain people could see this about me, but were too scared or too polite to pull my card. The deepest problem with *Bomb the Suburbs* is what you see when you turn my critiques of others around on me.

One of *Bomb the Suburbs'* big themes is the importance of choosing your target. You can't just knock down whatever two-bit tyrant stumbles onto your path. You have to trace power to its source to find its weak spots. Most of *Bomb the Suburbs* is spent attacking the wrong targets.

Look who my villains were: gangster rappers, rap journalists, petty white liberals, graffiti writers, record company execs, the CTA (Chicago Transit Authority), mean police, suburbanites, drivers who wouldn't pick me up hitch-hiking, and editors who wouldn't publish my book.

Look who my villains weren't: Corporate robber barons; prison, military, and highway profiteers; suburban developers; tollways, zoning boards and ass-kissing architects; covert drug-running CIA democracy destroyers; agribusiness and industrial super-polluters; rainforest axers; natural resource suckers; global media kingpins; their accomplices in the academy, philanthropy, law, and government; and the people who hire the editors who won't publish my book.

I let the big-time villains slide! I let them slide because they didn't seem that interesting at the time. I didn't even know who they were. To find out would have required research. The big villains were faceless and I couldn't do anything about them anyway. The only villains I could do something about were the small-fry villains who happened to have crawled onto my plate.

I poured ketchup on them and stabbed them with my fork.

MY IMPOSSIBLE DREAM

Hemingway said, "There's no use writing anything that's been written before unless you can beat it." If you have an allergy as I do to writing anything you know has been written before, there are three options left

1) Become a great writer like Hemingway.
2) Stick to minor themes no one else bothers with, or
3) Don't read.

In *Bomb the Suburbs,* I mostly stuck to two and three. That's why *Bomb the Suburbs* is an inner-city book which omits poverty, drugs, gangs, death, pain and violence, a book about race relations which ignores systemic racism, or anyone who isn't either white or black. A book about hip-hop that barely mentions music or dance, fashion or style. A book about people which for the most part omits family, love, sex, relationships, school, work, God, politics, and religion. A book for young people with no cars, fights, video games, TV, movies, sports, work or school. An intellectual work lacking foundation in history. A social criticism which doesn't deal with class, gender, sexual preference, corporate hegemony or the Internet. A supposedly bold book which timidly avoids most of life's big issues. A hypocritical book about few of the things it appears to be about, neither hot topics of the day nor great themes of human life.

The original meaning of "Bomb the Suburbs" had been to tell graffiti writers to stop fucking up the city. As the audience expanded, and I started having to explain myself to non-hip-hop people, I didn't know what to say. I hadn't done enough research to really criticize the suburbs, and the last thing I wanted to tell them was some hip-hop shit they could dismiss as a cute youth trend. So *Bomb the Suburbs* was reinvented as an all-encompassing metaphor for breaking down cliques in American life.

Mental suburbs was a great theme because it applied to everyone. I had a big mouth, but it was toothless. The material in the book hadn't caught up with my rhetoric. It still only spoke to my five or six original audiences. For the majority of Americans, Henry Hotel Clerk who likes history and heavy metal or Marsha Mechanic who's into movies and mountain bikes, *Bomb the Suburbs* sounded like another annoying suburb—or ghetto, more likely— which had nothing to do with them.

The most basic problem with *Bomb the Suburbs* (and why most people have trouble relating to it) is that its underlying theme is not struggle, but *affluence* and how to use it. And although most Americans are affluent relative to others, we tend not to view ourselves that way.

My defense to myself was that no matter the shortcomings of the book's content, at least it was reaching young people who didn't otherwise read. This was becoming less and less the case. I hadn't figured out how to get any black distributors, and outside Chicago the audiences were smaller, older and 80% white.

It's hard to write a book for both halves of a segregated society.

And to get older people in power to take you seriously.

Without losing the young whippersnapper I used to be.

Hence I change lanes back and forth in my audience, mixing metaphors, writing on both sides of the fence.

One day last spring, my roommate and I were talking about freight-hopping and where we wanted to hop to that summer. I said, "You know that story in the book about how we hopped that freight to New York . . . "

He said, "Story? What story? That was in the book?!?"

This is my roommate. We've known each other ten years. He's a brilliant rapper. He loves words. He is exactly the kind of person *Bomb the Suburbs* was written for. The book had been out for six months. Our apartment was littered with it. He had been selling the book at work.

If my own roommate wasn't reading the book, who was? I had spent two years on the book so far. I began to ask myself what I was really trying to do, and whether writing books or starting a community center was the best way to do it.

After a few exciting months, the Vision Village was becoming a minor disaster—the same minor disaster most community-minded people dream up, whether it's a business, a publication or an organization. We were starting an institution to unite and nurture people. But we hadn't done that first ourselves.

The doorbell and telephone rang day and night when they weren't disconnected. People weren't coming there to "unite" with people unlike themselves and they weren't reading the books in our library. People were coming there to see friends, do supposedly creative things they already knew how to do and to highlight the experience by smoking a blunt. By the end, it had become a shantytown dungeon, dark and dirty with dog mess, and refugees of every reason camping out in the common room. One of them called it a "hip-hop halfway house."

Fifteen-year-old Isaiah Dalton, one of the regulars at the Village, talented in three or four areas, was beaten into a coma in his West Side neighborhood. He had started hanging out there again as the situation at the Village began to deteriorate. If I had found a benefactor or employed better business tactics, I could've paid Isaiah to run the place and maybe he wouldn't have had to spend the summer in a coma.

Not that it's my fault. Just that life's mundane successes or failures are sometimes suddenly linked to survival or death. The average person in an average life span has the opportunity to save or cut short many lives, and I realized, if I factored in my linkages as a consumer, stockholder, worker, taxpayer, and citizen to the sweatshops, rainforests and military dictatorships of the world, I was probably ruining a lot more than I was saving.

Before I moved to the Vision Village, my goal had been to become a walking Vision Village. I spent my free time going to other people's neighborhoods, reading other people's books, and listening to other people. Now everyone was coming to my house, reading my book, working on my projects and listening to me. My success and notoriety as a writer had the paradoxical effect of reducing my effectiveness as an organizer.

As a child of the mass media, I never questioned my addiction to fame. I just wanted more of it. Jail takes away your freedom. Fame flatters you into giving it up. The more you do what you're supposed to do when you're a semi-recognized person (like answering the phone and opening your mail), the less you devote to the learning processes that made you worth listening to in the first place. Instead of continuing to develop my ignorant ass, I had tried to institutionalize and codify what I already knew.

A thousand people had come to the book release party for *Bomb the Suburbs,* so I had expected 3000 for the Bomb The Ghettos writing contest. Fewer than 500 people showed up, and at the end of the summer, only 20 entries were submitted to the contest. Most of the writers I knew, even people who had been at the festival, didn't submit anything, even though I personally reminded them to. I ended up giving out $2,000 of my own money, so many people were deserving.

There won't be a "Bomb the Ghettos" contest this year [1996]. I am too young (and not quite rich enough) to be throwing contests instead of reading and learning myself. I don't like the idea of contests, something I didn't realize until I threw one (I thought I just didn't like other people's contests, mine was gonna be different.) The contest put me in the position of playing God, and contestants in the position of trying to win by some other fool's standards.

TRIPLE CONSCIOUSNESS

I knew I was doing things wrong. I was desperate for criticism but I usually didn't know what to do when I got it. My friend Amanda kept telling me we had to make the writers' meetings less centered on me. I agreed. I tried pulling people aside and encouraging them to take over. I tried delegating responsibility. I tried giving away responsibility. I tried not showing up to meetings. Sometimes it worked. Ultimately, it didn't. As long as we were pursuing my dreams—as much as I felt they were our dreams—it was impossible to center on anyone other than me. The writers workshops died the week I left on tour.

I wanted desperately to be part of a team. I never knew whether to say "I" or "we," "my" or "our." Since I never searched hard for mentors, I always got myself into situations where I was the mentor.

One after another, the "bombs" were blowing up in my face. Most of my friendships were in disrepair. The hypocrisy of my public and private lives became unbearable and *Bomb the Suburbs* took on a sour meaning in our house. My roommates barely even said good-bye when I left for the "Bet With America." They were relieved I was gone.

Now you've heard the elevated side and the subway side of the story. When the State Street subway emerges on the South Side at 16th Street, it continues on to 95th street at ground level. I've been a subway person and an elevated person. Now I want to be a grounded person. Call it "Triple Consciousness." Not until you've glimpsed Heaven and Hell can you appreciate Earth.

The first two questions in life are whether we're sacred creatures and whether everything we do matters. The third question is how to be effective in a complex system where every action has tainted motives, side-effects, opportunity costs and backlash.

I went jogging with my dad the other day. He's a professor at the University of Chicago. I asked him how many mentors he's had in life. He counted eight or nine.

"That's all?" I ask. "Do you ever feel narrow?"

"I've had a lot of mentors compared to most people,"" he says.

My dad says most professors he knows have only had four or five. Some even got away with one or two. That's why my dad is one of the broadest educated people at the University. He has taught in five departments.

But I find myself wondering what kind of person my father would be if instead of eight or nine mentors, he'd studied with 80 or 90, not just at the University but from all walks of life. I wonder what's the minimum number of mentors a person needs to even become aware of his or her potential in life. Most people my age say they don't have any role models. I figure I need at least three hundred. The lower the quality of the role models, the more of them you need. Maybe if they're really good, I could get away with fifty.

Does that sound like a foolish and impossible dream? Good. So was my last book. World War III could happen in our lifetime and the only thing that's going to prevent it, I think, is ordinary people fighting like Heaven and Hell for our foolish, impossible dreams. And then doing it again smarter when it blows up in our face.

THE COOL RICH KIDS MOVEMENT

HOW BREAK-DANCING
GOT ME INTO PHILANTHROPY

In Greek, the word philanthropy means love of humanity.

In English it means giving away money.

I first got interested in philanthropy when I was giving a talk at Oberlin College about white people's role in destroying the world. This student came up to me afterwards and said, "My dad is the president of a company and my family has shitloads of money and I think society is fucked up and I want to use my money to do something about it. I don't know how much I'm gonna inherit or when but I want to start thinking now about what I need to do. And not just with my family money. I'm good with computers and I know how to run a business. But I'm trying to figure out which would be more effective, dedicating my skills and my life directly to activism and organizing, or making a shitload of money and giving it away. What do you think I should do?"

I was speechless.

I didn't know what to tell him.

Around the same time, I was at a cocktail party—yes, a cocktail party—with my Uncle Jay, his partner Carolyn, and Ed Sacks, who, as the founder of Saxon Paint was a recognizable face in Chicago from his TV commercials. Mr. Sacks told me that he fell in love with break-dancing when it first got big in 1984 and he sponsored breakin' competitions all over the city, in dozens of housing projects and parks around Chicago. He said, "We gave prizes to the winners, and all the kids who participated got one of our little paint hats."

That's when it clicked for me.

"What *color* were the paint hats?" I said. "Were they white with little red checkers on them?"

"Why yes they were!" he exclaimed.

Holy shit. I had been to one of his break-dance competitions at a park near my house. I had been the white kid with the black kids, trying to do the centipede, and a little bit of footwork, having the time of my life—it was one of the most magical moments of my childhood.

I had gotten one of the hats, a white paint hat with red checkers.

At 11 years old, I thought I was taking part in a spontaneous gathering at a local park. I had no idea it was sponsored by Ed Sacks, the white old paint guy on TV. Suddenly hip-hop wasn't quite what I thought it was. Neither was philanthropy.

When I was in fourth grade, my private-school class put on the play

"Charlie and the Chocolate Factory," based on the popular children's book by Roald Dahl. In the story, Charlie and four other children win golden tickets to take a tour in the magical chocolate factory of the mysterious confectioner Willie Wonka. The factory for the children is a fun house of temptations, and the other four children, each one a caricature of spoiledness, one by one fall victim to their own excesses. They are poetically lured to their respective fates. Shrieking Veruca Salt tries to grab a treat and she and her father fall down a hole. Mike Teevee gets shrunken down and put on TV screen. Gum-smacking Violet Beauregard snatches a piece of experimental gum and blows up into a blueberry. And Gluttonous Augustus Gloop falls into the chocolate river.

Charlie, by contrast, is a humble boy who takes care of his grandparents and appreciates everything that is given to him. Charlie passes all of Willie Wonka's tests and by the end of the tour he is the only one of the five children left standing.

Willie Wonka turns to Charlie and confides that he's planning to retire and has selected Charlie as the appropriate heir to his factory.

When Ms. Kalk's fourth grade class put on this play, I got cast as Charlie. I feel like after that I *became* Charlie. The book was a metaphor for the way I came to see the world and the values and perspectives I took on. Poor people were noble. Rich people were spoiled. Poor people were warm, caring and experienced in life. Rich people were cold, sheltered and materialistic. Poor people were honest, sure of themselves and fun to be around. Rich people were phony, boring and confused.

I preferred to wear hand-me-down clothes and I used to beg my grandmother not to buy me Izod or Polo, clothes I considered too snobby. Growing up on the South Side of Chicago, in an affluent neighborhood that was surrounded by the ghetto, I would daydream naively about how great my life would be if only I'd had the opportunity to grow up in the Robert Taylor Homes nearby—the world's largest public housing project. In seventh grade, I transferred from my private prep school to a public school that was 90% black. Now I had two sets of friends.

I tried to bring my two worlds together but none of my efforts succeeded as much as I would have liked. In 1995, my friends and I had to shut down the Vision Village because we could no longer afford the $850 rent. If we'd even had a couple of thousand dollars to start with, we could have covered someone's rent to live there and take care of the place part-time. That would have solved a lot of our problems. It made me mad, when I thought about it. Here we were trying so hard to do good in our little corner of the world, and a couple of thousand dollars kept us from continuing it.

And if I, as an upper-middle-class white guy couldn't get $3000 to run a youth center, imagine how many less-privileged people had run into the same dead end. How many of them got burnt out or discouraged because of problems that a few thousand dollars could have solved? Money doesn't solve all problems, and it can definitely create problems of its own. But if you know what you're doing, then a little bit of money can mean the difference between success or failure, inspiration or burnout, survival or game over.

I began to wonder, "What's up with all these foundations that are supposedly giving people grants to do good in the world?" None of the grassroots people I knew seemed to be getting any grants.

That's how I got interested in money. Realizing how much the real world is not like *Charlie and the Chocolate Factory*. In real life, most people who are poor and noble get stepped on and burnt out. In real life, someone like Willie Wonka could never own a factory, and even if he did, Veruca Salt's Dad would probably acquire it through a leveraged buy-out, and all the Oompah-Loompahs would be downsized. They'd get arrested for being poor and end up as telemarketers working in prison, or be quarantined and deported by the INS.

IN DEFENSE OF RICH KIDS

My family never talked much about money, except to say that we were "middle-class . . . well maybe upper-middle-class." A few years ago, it became clear that both my parents and my grandmother had a lot more money than I realized. As an only child, I stood to inherit a nice chunk of it. I didn't know how much and I didn't know when. They did not want me to become spoiled or think I didn't have to work.

A lot of people will use this information to write me off. Oh, he's a rich kid. No wonder he could publish a book, probably with his parents' money. And why's he going around bragging about it? What is he, stupid? Some of us have to work for a living, etc.

You can hate me if you want to. I am the beneficiary of a very unfair system. The system gives me tons of free money for doing nothing, yet it forces you to work two and three jobs just to get out of debt.

On top of that, I have the nerve to sit up here and talk about it and—for some it will seem—to rub it in. Most rich people are considerate enough to shut their mouths and pretend they're struggling too. To get on TV talking about, "I got this on sale."

I didn't really have anyone to talk about it with. I knew a lot of the kids I had gone to school with were in a similar situation but we never discussed our family money, except in really strange ways like how broke we were and how those other rich people were so spoiled/lucky. Our judgments of them betrayed our own underlying shame.

And let's talk right now about motives. As soon as you bring up philanthropy, people want to talk about motives. "Is he doing this for the right reasons or is he just doing this to make himself feel good?" Well, let me tell you, I am definitely doing this to make myself feel good and—call me crazy—I believe doing what you feel good about is one of the right reasons.

Yes, I have the luxury to give my money away because I know I'm going to inherit more later in life. But don't come to me with this bullshit, "Oh, it's easy for you to give away your money because you're gonna inherit more later." If it's so easy, how come more rich people aren't doing it? How come Americans only give 2% to charity across the board, whether they are rich, poor, or middle-class? I usually give away 20-30% of my income every year. But I just got my first steady job, so this year, if you throw in the book, I'll probably be giving away more like 50%.

Hell no, I'm not some kind of saint who has taken a vow of poverty and is now sitting in judgment of you or anyone else's money decisions. But be aware, it's easy to criticize my actions when you don't have much money. If you were in my situation, who's to say you'd be any different from 99% of other rich people who keep it all for themselves. Or if they do give it away, it's to big colleges, big arts, big religion, or big service, supporting bureaucratic institutions that maintain systemic problems by treating symptoms and obscuring root causes.

Which brings me to the next very selfish reason for my philanthropy. I have a political agenda and my philanthropic "generosity" plus my sense of strategy gives me more philanthropic power to change the world than people with 50 times my income.

The deeper reason why I give away my money is because I love the world. Because I'm grateful to be alive at all. Because I'm scared about where we're headed. Because we owe it to our great-grandchildren. Because we owe it to the millions of years of evolution it took to get us here. And to everyone before us who fought to change history and make things as good as they are now. Because I know how to change history and I know it takes money. Because I get more joy out of making things better for everyone than I get out of making things materially better for myself. Because I know how to make and spend money on myself. It's boring. There's no challenge in it. And no love in it. I love helping good things happen, and supporting people I believe in. Especially people and organizations that have NO money put into them by traditional foundations and charities. I'm not talking about your everyday charities like diabetes or your college that already have multi-million dollar budgets set up to fight for them.

They're new.

They don't exist yet.

They're like diabetes in 1921, the year before they extracted insulin.

They're like your college the year before it was founded.

Don't get me wrong. My father has juvenile diabetes. And I love my college too. But the money supporting the Juvenile Diabetes Foundation, and my college is already so big, their fundraising operations so effective, that giving my money to them is a drop in the bucket.

For the organizing efforts I want to support, every dollar is like a seed, helping not only to create a new kind of organization, but an organization that will be copied and that decades from now will establish new fields of work. It is the most strategic way possible to change the course of history, and the most unpopular because it's so high-risk.

THE COOL RICH PEOPLE'S CONFERENCE

In the summer of 1997, I got a mysterious package in the mail. It contained a magazine called More Than Money Journal. The subtitle read, "Exploring the personal, political and spiritual impact of money in our lives." It also contained a brochure telling me about a conference in Seattle for "The Next Generation of Philanthropists." Yes, it's true, there is a decent-sized network of rich people who give a shit (future rich people in my case) who go to conferences and talk about their money. How to invest in more "socially responsible" companies and how to give it away. It is all very serious. An acquaintance of mine who'd had a hunch about my financial situation put me on their mailing list.

The conference offered "a safe space" for "people of wealth." I didn't know what to think of it all. Well, to be honest, I thought it was ridiculous. I couldn't picture myself sitting in a room with a bunch of rich people talking about money. I couldn't relate to it and it gave me the creeps. But deep down, I was intrigued.

So, like a good self-schooler, I went. I went expecting to meet all these clueless rich people who had no connection to the grassroots and no idea what they were doing. What I found instead blew my mind.

First of all, one of the women there was an old friend of mine, an environmental activist from Chicago who I never would have guessed was rich. Then there was Trish Millines, one of the few black millionaires at Microsoft. She used her money to start the Technology Access Foundation in Seattle for young people of color to learn computers. John Moyers was there, the son of TV host Bill Moyers. John is head of the Schumann Foundation, and he spoke passionately about funding organizations that fight to get big money out of politics.

The conference was amazing. People were friendly and down to Earth.

Everyone there was either doing amazing stuff or was trying to figure out how. I learned so much so fast. I learned that I have a lot to learn. I didn't know anything about financial planning or estate planning or the art and business of philanthropy. I just knew I wanted to use my money and my time to do extraordinary things. And I knew I wanted to help other young people make their impossible dreams come true.

The conference was a turning point for me. I realized that there were all these other rich people trying to figure out how to give their money away wisely. The idea is to support groups that work for "change not charity." We're not just going to put Band-Aids on the symptoms of social problems—we're going to go change the root causes that are creating the problems in the first place.

It makes sense.

You have to be more of a detective. You don't just say, "Oh, look at those flood victims on TV. Poor them. Aren't they unlucky/stupid for living there? Let's send money to the Red Cross so they can pile more sand bags."

Instead you are skeptical. You say, "Wait a minute, why are there so many more floods now than when I was growing up? Could it be that the auto industry, in cahoots with developers, construction unions, local zoning boards and the Federal Government have spent the last 50 years paving over America's open lands with subdivisions, roads and parking lots so that the water has nowhere else to go? What organizations are successfully fighting this? How can I support them?"

A whole world was opening up for me. The conference was put on by a foundation called A Territory Resource. ATR is part of a loose-knit network of renegade foundations around the country which were started by a small group of rich people in the 1960s and '70s. They come from a spectrum of backgrounds and use a variety of strategies. Some give specifically to grassroots efforts for social change. Some do socially responsible investing. Some fund micro-enterprise. Some put activists on their boards in order to share their decision-making power with the people on the ground.

Some, like Responsible Wealth, in Boston, fight against unfair government policies that benefit the rich, and use their stockholder status to introduce shareholder resolutions which challenge companies to stop using sweatshops or cancer-causing chemicals. (They need to add to their list the prison industry!)

One of the people I met at the ATR conference was Anne Slepian, one of the founders of the magazine *More Than Money*. She and her husband Christopher Mogil had been activists in West Philly when they unexpectedly inherited money. They went around interviewing all these other rich people who had done creative things with their money from Ben Cohen of Ben & Jerry's to George Pillsbury (of the Pillsbury Family) to Millard Fuller (founder of Habitat for Humanity) and a bunch of other incredible people most of us have never heard of. Phil Villers went to Harvard Business School and made

$80 million in computers just so he could give it away. Tracy Gary helped start dozens of organizations with her inheritance, including one of the first battered women's shelters in the U.S., and the San Francisco Women's Foundation, each of which became a model for countless similar organizations across the country.

Anne and Christopher turned the interviews into a book called *We Gave Away a Fortune*. They started an organization called More Than Money, (formerly The Impact Project), which works with rich people—especially new inheritors—to think creatively about their resources, and the personal dilemma of having more than others. They publish a journal called *More than Money* for socially-conscious rich people to share their stories. And they do theater and organize groups to get rich people talking about the unique options and dilemmas that come with having more money.

One organization, United For A Fair Economy which is the parent organization of Responsible Wealth, includes both rich and poor people. They employ a full time street artist, Andrew Boyd, who organizes hilarious stunts, like this one:

Today on the steps of the State House in Concord, New Hampshire, as Steve Forbes announced his candidacy for President, United for a Fair Economy launched its latest campaign, "Billionaires for Steve Forbes."

At first, UFE staffers and volunteers, smartly dressed in pinstripe suits and formal dresses, held innocuous signs and led supportive chants such as "Forbes in 2000," and "Run Steve Run!" A large hand-painted banner carried Forbes' slogan, HE WANTS YOU TO WIN.

However, each of the signs had another sign behind it. At the moment of his announcement, the large banner was pulled away to reveal another that read BILLIONAIRES FOR STEVE FORBES—BECAUSE INEQUALITY IS NOT GROWING FAST ENOUGH. Meanwhile, the hand-held signs suddenly read, TAX CUTS FOR US, NOT

OUR MAIDS, TAX WORK, NOT WEALTH, and FREE THE FORBES 400. What a lift he must have felt from his billionaire boosters as they chanted "Let workers pay the tax, so investors can relax," and other supportive slogans they had devised in his honor!

All major press were there: CBS, NBC, ABC, CSPAN and many others.

THE MOST EFFECTIVE THING YOU EVER DO

Small renegade grassroots foundations now operate in most areas of the country. In Chicago, we have the Crossroads Fund, which I recently found out was started by the parents of someone I went to school with. One of the other people on the Crossroads board of directors is the father of one of my friends I used to do graffiti with! I also learned that Crossroads gave a grant to the Autonomous Zone, which is an anarchist punk center down the street from the Vision Village and if we had applied to Crossroads for a grant, there's a good chance we could have gotten it!

The more I learned about philanthropy, the more I realized that practically every "grassroots" organization and community leader I had ever heard of gets a lot of their money from a very small number of cool rich people. Grassroots organizations don't usually like to talk about it. They talk about how they are of the people, by the people, for the people, and to a large extent that is true. They do depend on $25 contributions and the support of a wide base. But take away that one behind-the-scenes cool rich person and most of these grassroots organizations are fucked.

Every hell-raising magazine from *The Nation* to *Mother Jones* to *Adbusters* to *In These Times* to *The Progressive* depend for their survival on half a dozen cool rich people. It was a hard lesson to learn. But it filled me with hope. What if we could double the number of cool rich people who are funding social change from say five hundred to a thousand? Then we could double the number of organizers on the street, lawyers in the court rooms, lobbyists in Congress. Double the number of investigative reporters. There are so many people who want to do progressive work who can't because there aren't enough activist jobs. People come out of law school to become environmental lawyers and they end up having to defend corporations because they have to pay off their student loans. Environmental groups can't afford to hire them. The same goes for radical artists and journalists, forced to get jobs in advertising and public relations.

Five hundred more cool rich people could change all that.

Five hundred cool rich people could change the political landscape of this country.

Now don't get me wrong. I'm not saying philanthropy will solve all our problems, especially not the way 99% of it is done now. I'm not saying cool rich people are any more important or worthy than any other people. Poor people are made to feel like they aren't worth anything and that's wrong. I don't want to feed into that by focusing on rich people for a while. We need billions of people from billions of backgrounds trying billions of strategies to save this planet. It's just that every serious effort to change things takes people with money who understand how to support a movement. All these naive college or punk or hip-hop revolutionaries talking about, "Fuck that. I don't know any rich people and if I do they're assholes and anyway, I don't need their money." I only have one thing to say. Wait until your community center gets shut down. Wait until your broke grassroots genius friends start burning out because they have to do menial shit all day because they don't have the time or capital to make their dreams come true.

Consider these statistics. There are about five million millionaire households in the U.S. That's approximately one out of every 50 people. So, if you are a social person (not a hermit) and you are not currently serving a life sentence in prison, then chances are you will have the opportunity at some point in your life to get to know a number of people who are, at the very least, millionaires. Most of the time you will not know they are millionaires. Half of the time, millionaires don't even realize they are millionaires. My parents didn't realize they were. People usually have their assets tied up in many different forms such as houses, trusts, mutual funds, stocks, bonds and retirement accounts.

Less than 1% of all charitable giving ends up in the hands of people who are working to change the system. As Teresa Odendahl has pointed out in her ironically-titled book *Charity Begins at Home,* contrary to popular belief, most charity money does not go to help poor children help themselves. The vast majority of money goes to big churches, big colleges, big hospitals, big arts and social service organizations which either directly cater to privileged people, or which treat the symptoms of social ills without ever addressing the root causes.

Guess what America's #1 charity is?

Harvard University.

This is why:

Let's say you're a Harvard alum.

Guess how many people Harvard employs in its development office whose job it is to get your money away from you?

About 250.

And that's just for the college. If you include all the graduate programs, it's more like 400. Four hundred people whose job it is to get your money away from you. And the other big colleges and universities and museums are not far behind. They do research on you, find out how much money you have, find out anything they can about your life, what else you've given money to, what your hobbies and political views and personal quirks are.

Fundraising is a very creepy profession to me. As they say in the funding world, it's all about relationships. You want to build a relationship with me so that you can convince me to give you my money? Sounds like a really great relationship, just the kind I want to have. Fundraising, like PR, is a very manipulative profession. Be careful what you want to hear, because if you have the bucks, they're gonna tell it to you.

There has never been a really good journalistic exposé of the fundraising nonprofit philanthropy world. Journalists, do you want to win a Pulitzer prize? Do you want to be blacklisted forever from getting a grant? I'm telling you, there's a whole world out there no one has done a good job of writing about. Everyone who is close enough to really know its inner-workings is in on it. Everyone on the outside who should be concerned is clueless. I try to talk to my friends about philanthropy and no one knows what I'm talking about. I can't write the exposé because I'm in on it too.

Between public relations and fundraising, we're creating a nation of slick people. My thing is:

A) I don't want to be manipulated, and

B) I want to give my money to the places that will use it to save the world for our children and grandchildren.

Greenpeace, the giant environmental organization has only ten people in their entire development department. LISTEN, the urban youth leadership organization I work for in D.C. doesn't even have one. My boss Lisa Sullivan fundraises, runs the organization, and does a fifty million other things on the side. Imagine how different the world would be if organizations like ours working to save the world had 400 people whose sole job it was to raise money. Then we could have hundreds of thousands of people actually in the field doing the work.

Then we might actually have a fighting chance. Over the next 50 years, the upper-classes of my generation stand to inherit or earn the greatest personal fortune in history, while the lower classes both here and internationally will continue slipping deeper into poverty and debt.

That's where the Cool Rich Kids Movement comes in. Actually there isn't much of a "Cool Rich Kids Movement." That's just what I call the loose-knit network of maybe 100 of us young people with wealth who are in conversation with each other, and who support each other in taking small but significant actions. We are asking our parents to teach us about money. We are helping our families make responsible decisions about investments. Some of us are getting on the boards of family foundations or helping our families to start them. We introduce each other to amazing grassroots people to break the isolation of wealth. We are just in the process of getting organized. We had our first conference last spring, sponsored by the Third Wave Foundation in New York. More are planned.

My goal is to get more young people with wealth in on the conversation. With five million millionaires in the U.S., even if we only spoke to the coolest 1% of all millionaire kids, that's still 50,000 people!

One half of the money I give away every year goes directly to grassroots youth activist organizations that I have a relationship with. (No, I don't make them kiss up to me. I just give it to them, thank them for their hard work and if they feel funny about it, I remind them that the only reason I have the money in the first place is because I've been so privileged and so many people have helped me. So it wasn't really "my" money to begin with. Often times I have to *insist* that people take my money. We've all had so many bad experiences.)

The other half of my money I donate to organizing people with wealth.

That may seem strange at first.

Why give money to people who already have wealth?

From all my experience with grassroots organizations, I believe that organizing people with wealth is the most powerful work I do. And paradoxically, it is some of the hardest work to fundraise for because everybody including rich people thinks, "Why give rich people more money?" And that's why only a few dozen people in America have the job of helping rich people figure out how to come to terms with and do cool things with their money.

I think we need more of those people in the world.

So recently, I've changed my focus in a big way.

I joined the board of More Than Money. I am helping to start the Active Element Foundation, which is the first foundation that will specifically work with young donors on funding grassroots youth activism. And I'm also helping to start the Self-Education Foundation, which will tap successful people who either didn't like school or who dropped out to fund self-education resource centers which will support poor kids to take learning into their own hands. I am helping to organize a series of conferences around the country for young people with wealth, put on by The Third Wave Foundation and the Comfort Zone, which you'll read about here later.

I believe the most effective thing I do for the world every year is to buy gift subscriptions of *More Than Money Journal* for my privileged friends and to keep a ready supply of *Money Talks. So Can We.* for every cool young person I meet who has money. This is the most effective action I do. Any other possible action I could do, one cool rich person could hire ten more people to take my place.

But there's very little room in our culture to talk about having money and funding renegade work. Most rich people be like, "See you later." And most grassroots people be like, "It's easy for you because you're rich." There's resentment either way. People who aren't rich can play a huge role supporting us. So many of my friends who aren't wealthy act like, "Ha ha ha, going to your rich kids conference." That's not going to make me want to talk to you. If you are truly down to change the world, don't try to score points by alienating your rich friends with snide remarks. If you take the time to truly understand us and support us as people, more than likely, we will do the same for you. Rich people don't choose to be born rich any more than poor people choose to be born poor. The sickness of our society damages us each in different and complicated ways, and we sometimes forget that rich people get damaged too. Not just in a mocking way, like, "Oh, they're so spoiled." But in a real way. One of the most common ways privileged people get damaged is that we are taught not to talk about money. We put a wall around ourselves, and then it is hard for us to be honest with people who aren't rich. This makes us cold and creates a vicious cycle of not trusting and not sharing ourselves or our money.

There are only a few of us out here doing this work, which is why I have been thrust into the spotlight. It's a little ridiculous actually that I am speaking for rich kids when I haven't even inherited my money yet. But there was a deafening silence and someone needed to come out here and give us a bold public voice. Do you have any cool rich friends who may be looking for people in similar situations to talk to?

Hint: You do.

Please please please pass this along to them.

It just might be the most effective thing you ever do.

An Interview with Tracy Hewat
MONEY TALKS. SO CAN SHE.

So how does it feel to be the only person in the country whose full-time job is to help young rich people do good with money?

Ha! God, I wonder if that's true.

Tracy, you're it. Who else is there?

I don't know. I wonder if there are people we don't know who are working through organizations we don't know. Hopefully, we'll become enough of a center to attract those people or to hear about those people.

So you suspect there are others?

I do think there are other people who share at least a part of what we're doing. I heard someone on National Public Radio who does money management and does outreach and classes specifically for young people. I sent him a copy of *Money Talks. So Can We.* and I tried to call him but he never called me back. I may well be the only person doing it who's not selling a service, but there may be other people who are doing it for a fee.

Yeah, but that taints it. And for a lot of rich people who are afraid of being used, it's an issue of trust flat out. That you're not just one more person who wants something. This is a labor of love for you. You're not drawing any salary off of it. It's important for people to talk freely about their personal demons with money, because a lot of times that's what blocks you from being more generous with what you have . . .

My hope is that people will have enough information and develop enough confidence with money that they'll be able to make active decisions about . . . really about how they want to live their lives at all levels and how they want to participate in social change. But I realize I'm not answering the question you originally asked me.

About being the only one?

Yeah [laughing].

So how does it feel?

Lonely. Under-skilled. Under-experienced. Excited.

How do you explain what you're doing to people who don't know anything about philanthropy or social change or . . . .Do you even have conversations like that with people?

All the time. Talking about it seems like a huge opportunity to me, to make people think about things in ways they've probably never thought about them before. About wealthy people. About progressive social change and how it happens and who's doing it. Because most people's assumption is that wealthy people would not work against the system that benefits them.

So when people say, "What do you do," you know . . . "I'm a lawyer, I'm a teacher, I'm an electrician . . . " What do you say?

I direct a little nonprofit called Resource Generation. We encourage young people in their twenties with either earned or inherited wealth to get good information about their resources and we work to connect them early with the progressive philanthropic networks and with each other.

But what about people who say, "What's philanthropy?" "What's social change?" "You mean rich people doing what?" "Network of progressive what?"

Sometimes I get someone like that, like when I make cold calls to colleges . . .

You make cold calls?

Yeah.

What do you ask?

I ask, "Who are considered the most progressive faculty members?"

You ask that?

Yes. I usually ask to speak to the head of Women's Studies. I always speak to the chaplain. I should be speaking to someone in the counseling department but if none of those leads turns up anything, then maybe I'll call the sociology department and ask for anyone who teaches a sociology course that deals with class.

Oh, clever.

We're smart cookies.

How many colleges have you contacted people at?

Probably twenty. I've only really talked to people at a handful. But we're working on doing more. We're temporarily slowed down in our outreach because we're building an organizational structure that will support us in doing larger and more directed outreach.

What are the responses you get?

I've certainly been asked how can I claim that I'm working toward economic justice if I'm not personally giving away my fortune. I was meeting with the director of another organization who was a young woman who had started her own organization, and I was meeting with her because I wanted to hear her insight on that. That was one of the first questions she asked me, it was a testing. People want to test the motives of wealthy people generally.

What did you say?

A couple things: I do in fact give away a huge amount annually. I try to give strategically. I was grateful for my fortune. And call me selfish, I was not going to give it all away. But I had another contribution in the work that I was doing. I had come to speak to her about that contribution in hopes that she would support me in working toward a more just world—economic justice to help the organizations we both believe in who are working for social change.

What was her organization?

A very wonderful organization that supports girls, particularly low-income girls, and they don't have money and she's putting her blood, sweat and tears into keeping it afloat.

What other responses do you get?

A lot of people will say, "Isn't that funny! My roommate in college was wealthy and we never talked about it." Or, "My cousin just married someone who's wealthy." Or . . .

"Can I talk to you in private?"

Yes! With some regularity, people say, "You know, I inherited some money and I never told anyone. You're the first person I've told."

Wow.

The people we're speaking to—young, wealthy, socially conscious—are frequently isolated and are very excited to find information directed at them and a group of people that can relate to their situation. It's a situation with some apparent contradictions. There's no question about it. And I think those of us who count ourselves among that group, either we ignore the contradictions or we....there are certainly people who become paralyzed by the contradictions.

Or destroyed, like with cocaine and stuff.

And paralyzed is a form of being destroyed. Or else you acknowledge that there are contradictions, and you realize that even within those contradictions, you still have many opportunities to make a positive impact, and to learn from your peers, and to join with your peers in a multitude of different actions.

Tell me some stories.

Well, one young woman comes to mind. She was an international student here in this country and I met her because one of her teachers realized she was an extremely wealthy young woman and suggested she take an internship in New York City in lieu of her final year of college. She had quite a frank conversation with the woman she was interning with—who called me in a panic. I sent her our resource guide, *Money Talks. So Can We.* I met with her. She had taken this semester in New York to learn all she could about socially responsible investing, venture capital, community development.

She was about to be seated on a number of very influential boards. She will in her lifetime control—I didn't ask how much, that wasn't the point of the conversation—she will control significant wealth directly and significant wealth through a foundation. On one of the boards she will serve on with her siblings, she'll be the eldest. And she said a number of things to me that were particularly poignant given how powerful she is. One being that . . . none of her friends knew how wealthy she is because she was afraid it would influence their friendships. In the past, she had had people visit her in one of the many homes she had grown up in and it changed the way they related toward her. A number were intimidated. A number had very strained relationships with her after that.

She is, by the way, completely down-to-earth. She's very smart, and wise, but I also think really alone with the responsibility for this money and I saw her really working to do the right thing, to get as much information as she could, to make good and well-informed decisions, to be socially conscious. And I saw her doing it without the support of her friends. She said, "Rather than going back to serve on the board, I'd rather go live with my boyfriend, but my father insists that I go serve on the board." I put her in touch with other people who'd served on the boards of large family foundations.

I think of her a lot. Over and over again she said, "I have no right to complain. I have no right to complain. I have been so blessed in my life." And I thought in that moment how brave and honorable she was, and how scary it was for anyone of any age or background to have that much responsibility. We feel we have no right to have difficulties, which is such a funny thing if you think about it, because while money does alleviate certain difficulties, it doesn't alleviate others.

Yeah, like after survival, most of the important ones, like love . . .

Death.

Living in a way you can be proud of . . .

And she's an example of someone who might well be frozen and incapacitated by the enormity of the money and the learning curve and she's not at all frozen and she's taking the steps she needs to make good decisions.

She didn't learn it from her family?

Not about the progressive side of it certainly. Clearly she didn't know enough about what the options were and what steps she was taking with this money. I found her very inspiring. I hope I meet many people like her in this work and support them to use their money like the tool that it is.

What do you tell people who are really interested? Like say you meet someone who's young and knows their family has money . . .

If they want to know more, I'll go on and say it's not just about philanthropy, but also socially-responsible investing, community investing, investing in screened companies, or investing in non-screened companies and doing shareholder activism, speaking publicly, getting involved in organizations you believe in, sitting on boards, volunteering your time, using your name . . . .

You mean recognizable names like DuPont or Rockefeller?

Yeah, or making your name recognizable by using your money, using your connections, leveraging your resources, using your talents, talking to your family and friends—or whichever of the three billion ways that you as a wealthy person can engage in social change.

This is what you encourage people to do.

Or smaller stuff. You might be twenty and not be in a position where you're comfortable giving a huge amount. You may not be comfortable being a shareholder activist, but you may be comfortable to sit down with members of your family or friends or friends of the family and ask questions or influence their money decisions. You may be able to encourage other people to be proactive with their money before you become proactive with yours. And maybe somewhere down the road you'll try signing your name on a fundraising letter of an organization you believe in, and sending it out to five people you know and making follow-up calls, or not making follow-up calls. Just sending it out.

Yeah, I love the way you're all about options. And recognizing what different places people are in.

My role is not to tell people what to do with their money. I tell people, "Here are the arguments I've heard people make. Here are the range of options. How can I support you in making the best decisions?"

Cool Rich Kids Movement Resources

- Active Element Foundation 532 LaGuardia Pl. PMB #510 New York, NY 10012 (www.activelement.org)
- Third Wave Foundation 116 E. 16th St. New York, NY 10003, 212-388-1898 (www.thirdwavefoundation.org)
- Resource Generation/*Money Talks. So Can We.* PO Box 400336 Cambridge, MA. 02140, 617-441-5567 (www.resourcegeneration.org)
- Responsible Wealth/United for A Fair Economy 37 Temple Pl. 2nd Fl. Boston MA 02111, 617-423-2148 (www.responsiblewealth.org)
- More Than Money 21 Linwood St. Arlington, MA 02474, 781-648-0776 (www.morethanmoney.org)
- Grassroots Fundraising Journal/Chardon Press PO Box 11607 Berkeley, CA 94701, 510-704-8714, www.chardonpress.com
- Self Education Foundation PO Box 30790 Philadelphia PA 19104, 215-235-4379 dropout@forpresident.com (www.selfeducation.org)
- Adventure Philanthropy (www.adventurephilanthropy.net)
- National Network of Grantmakers 1717 Ketner Blvd #110 San Diego, CA 92101, 619-231-1348 (www.nng.org)
- Social Venture Network PO Box 29221 San Francisco, CA 94129, 415-561-6501 (www.svn.org)

HOMESCHOOLING
AND SELF-EDUCATION

SCHOOLAHOLICS ANONYMOUS

Are you a young person who's still in school?

Then I have a dare for you.

No, let's not call it a *dare*—we don't want to scare your parents.

Let's call it a *sociology experiment.*

When you go in to school on Monday, ask all your teachers to name one thing they learned in school that they *still use* that they couldn't have learned on their own.

Be polite. Say, "Excuse me Ms. Jones but if school is so *important,* can you please name *one* thing *you* learned in school that you couldn't have learned on your own?"

You should ask all adults this question.

It should be interesting to see what they come up with.

Because if they do come up with something then the next question is, why couldn't they learn it on their own? Weren't they resourceful enough? Did they have problems with self-motivation? And then the next question is, What in the hell are they doing teaching *you?* And, why in hell are you listening? Isn't there something *better* you could be doing with your time? And if there is, then what in the hell are you still doing in school?

I have been asking myself this question since I was about ten. But by the time I finally decided once and for all to quit school I was already halfway through college. What possessed me to stay in school for ten extra years when I knew I had better things to do?

It's because school is like a drug. Okay when used in moderation but too much of it can cause damaging side effects, including passivity, dullness, emotional dependency, rebelliousness, anti-social behavior, mood swings, disorientation, impaired judgment, eating disorders, depression, self-hatred, and dislike of learning. Except that school is even more dangerous than conventional drugs because it is a socially acceptable addiction forced onto children too young to realize they have any other choice. School serves as a "gateway drug" to other kinds of addictions such as alcoholism, smoking, sex addiction, delinquency, materialism, workaholism, heroin, cocaine and coffee. There needs to be a Surgeon General's warning on schools the same way they have it on cigarettes.

Somebody needs to start up Schoolaholics Anonymous. I wish there had been a Schoolaholics Anonymous chapter in my school!

Hello.

My name is Billy. I am psychologically addicted to school.

Up until 6th grade, I loved my teachers and I loved school. I was interested in everything. I loved math and science and reading and social studies. By the end of 6th grade, I hated math and science and social studies. I was bored in all my classes. I thought I was stupid. I thought my teachers were idiots. And I had lost all interest in reading. I couldn't even write a simple article for the school newspaper. The only things I was interested in were girls, adventure, and sneaking around the city writing graffiti.

In 10th grade I got a job in a library shelving magazines and books. I began reading about graffiti, which was the only subject I still had much interest in. That got me back into reading again and now I am one of those lucky people who actually makes a living as a writer. I have tried to quit school three times. I worked odd jobs, did internships, started a small business, won research grants and awards as a professional journalist, threw parties, did grassroots organizing, edited a newspaper and a book, published another book, organized a conference of five hundred people, ran a youth center, made friends in almost every neighborhood in my hometown Chicago and hitchhiked around the country twice to every major city except Dallas. I had a life. I did not need school. But school still had this strange grip on me. I was experiencing withdrawal.

THE UNIVERSITY OF PLANET EARTH

Part of the trap is that I was now in college. Everyone knows high school is a waste of time but college is considered a great privilege. I loved college. I felt at home there. I had free food, my own room, no responsibilities. My tuition was even free because my Dad's a professor. It would be stupid for me to quit now. I'd be throwing away privileges, not just free tuition but the acceptance of my family, future employers, and mates. And my Jewish grandmother. What in the hell was I supposed to tell her?

Never mind that she, the least "educated" member of our family, has become the most financially successful. Never mind that my other most "successful" relative—William Horberg, a big-time Hollywood producer *(Sliding Doors, In Search of Bobby Fisher)*—is also a college dropout.

In my grandmother's mind, the only two respectable things a young person can do is work or go to school. There is no third alternative. There's no such thing as "I learn on my own, find my own teachers, create my own work." Abraham Lincoln, Florence Nightengale, Frank Lloyd Wright, Malcolm X, Joan of Arc and Benjamin Franklin are from a different universe. They are from History—things were different back then. And how dare you imply you're in a category with them?

To me, they were just people who lived as they believed, did what they loved, faced up to the challenges of their time, and happened to become famous. Great and terrible things would happen in my lifetime also. Was I prepared to do my part?

When I was 14, my hero was a rapper named KRS-One who had dropped out of 8th grade and educated himself. When I informed my parents that I intended to do the same, they told me it was illegal, and they would send me to an all boys military school if I tried. Having spent my life in school where everything is spoon-fed, I was not even resourceful enough to find out that they were wrong. And in retrospect, maybe I was a little bit scared. Okay, I was very scared. But as I became more resourceful, and learned about the possibilities available to me, I gained confidence to take my education into my own hands. Self-education is an upward spiral that way. I had already found a love of magazines, an ease with talking to strangers, and the essential ingredient of any self-education—the habit of asking questions. So one summer day three years ago, I was in a little bookstore in Portland, Oregon called Reading Frenzy and I asked the owner, Chloe Eudaly, what her favorite books were.

She didn't even have to think about it.

"That one!" she said. She pointed to a self-published book with crude red and green illustrations. Its title? *The Teenage Liberation Handbook: How to Quit School and Get a Real Life and Education* by Grace Llewellyn.

"I'm not a teenager," was my first thought, and I already have a real life and education, thanks anyway (I was preparing to enter my Junior year of college—which I loved—and I already knew how to educate myself outside of school.) Besides, if Grace Llewellyn was so self-educated, how come her book looked so amateurish and why hadn't I heard of it before—why hadn't she educated herself in design and marketing? In retrospect, maybe I was a little bit threatened. Okay, I was very threatened. But I bought the book anyway as a gift for a friend.

I started reading it and the gift was to me—I was really moved and when I returned to college in the fall, it felt like coasting. I had big plans and the things I needed most there were no classes for. Hello? There are no sex classes. No friendship classes. No classes on how to navigate a bureaucracy, build an organization, raise money, create a database, buy a house, love a child, spot a scam, talk someone out of suicide, or figure out what was important to me. Not knowing how to do these things is what mess people up in life, not whether they know Algebra or can analyze literature.

What if the way some of us learn best is the opposite of the way we were taught to learn in school? And what if the things you most want to do in life aren't considered a career? There's no career called walking around the street helping homeless people. You have to get a job at a social service agency where you'll have to spend most of your time faxing, filling out forms and applying for grants. That's a *crime*. That's the indirect, bureaucratic, unsatisfying, ineffective, busy work way of living taught to us in school. Self-education, in contrast, is direct, pertinent, powerful, and fun. I wanted a self-education that freed up my imagination to see how things could be changed.

I didn't want to write any more papers proving I could read two books and compare them. I wanted to make giant charts to compare everything that mattered to me.

I didn't want to memorize a bunch of facts and forget them. I wanted to know facts I could use and organize them like an almanac in a way I could whip out on any fool who tried to test me.

I didn't want to speed through assigned texts. I wanted to read some carefully, others not at all.

I didn't want to rush my diary. I wanted to write down everything important and organize it like a bible for instant consultation.

I didn't want to hear about amazing people. I wanted to meet them, apprentice with them, be their partner.

I didn't want to sit in classrooms. I wanted to see the world.

I looked at my friends who graduated college. Most of them are paying off debts now, riding the conveyor belt into graduate school, and selecting their mates from unnecessarily narrow pools. They are mid-life crises waiting to happen. Or maybe they won't even have mid-life crises. Maybe they'll just get stuck. Geniuses at following directions, they have little direction of their own. They're good at fitting into structures but they have little idea how to change one. They may be brilliant in their narrow fields, but they're kind of dim about the big picture. Some of them feel their narrow field *is* the big picture. They have no idea whether they'd be happier doing something else.

I prefer to have my mid-life crises now—early and often. I quit college in the middle of my Junior year and enrolled as a student at The University of Planet Earth, the world's oldest and largest educational institution. It has billions of professors, tens of millions of books, and unlimited course offerings. Tuition is free. There are no degrees and no one ever graduates.

Students pose their own questions and design their own curriculum.

Here is my question:

How can I commit the most good and the least evil in my lifetime?

Here is my curriculum:

"Live in a different place every year: D.C., Oakland, New York, L.A., a farm, and somewhere in the South. Play a different sport every day of the week, preferably with a different ethnic group: Basketball with blacks, martial arts with Chinese, capoeira with Brazilians, soccer with some of everyone, tennis with WASPs, etc. Every Sunday attend a different place of worship. Every day get to know someone new. Volunteer, attend lectures, talk to strangers on the street. Seek out hundreds of role models and mentors. The rest of the time, go to the library, read whatever I want, take notes and make charts. Create my own personal bible, almanac and telephone book. For discipline, live in high-crime neighborhoods. That ought to keep a gun to my head. Save up enough to travel to a different continent each year; otherwise, work as little as possible. Do that for five years. That will be my freshman survey course. Then I'll have a better idea of what to do as a sophomore."

I haven't followed my curriculum exactly. I keep changing it as opportunities arise. I had to scale back some of my goals because I needed to make money. My parents wouldn't use college money to help me educate myself and I got depressed for a while because I felt like they had no faith in me or my decisions in life. But self-education is the all-purpose fixer. It really can get you out of anything and into anything else. Recently, I researched my way into a dream job where I'll be paid to do almost exactly what I planned to do anyway —so I have to say that so far my self-education is going pretty well. My only regret is that I didn't start earlier.

Eventually, I'm gonna make a living as a public interest consultant. You say you've never heard of a "public interest consultant"? Oh, you will. I'm gonna be one. You're gonna be able to come to me in about five years. If you want to turn your nose up at me because I don't have a college degree—fine, your loss. I'm gonna know everything, and more importantly, everyone. Maybe someday I'll regret quitting school. Maybe I started too late. Maybe I won't be a good enough consultant and maybe my plans won't fly. But I have to try. As Grace Llewellyn writes, "The only alternative to making mistakes is for someone else to make all your decisions for you, in which case you will make their mistakes instead of your own."

THE UNSCHOOLING MOVEMENT

Grace Llewellyn and a few hundred other parents—mostly women—have been forming a loose-knit movement with hundreds of young "unschoolers" across the country who found out how to quit school legally and educate themselves by doing whatever they damn well please.

Sound fishy?

Let me tell you about a few of them.

Anna Fritz quit school when she was 15. She was a straight A student on her way to becoming class valedictorian at the School of the Arts in Milwaukee. Instead of taking music, she played professionally and studied with a renown cello teacher at University of Wisconsin at Madison. Instead of taking science, she apprenticed with a botanist at a museum greenhouse. Instead of taking English, she joined a critique group of professional writers. Instead of taking art or business, she worked at a photography studio. Instead of taking social studies, she worked as the organizer for Peace Action Milwaukee and represented the organization at the national meetings in Washington, D.C.

Kyla Wetherell quit school at 16 and decided to go to South America. Not as part of some foreign exchange program but on her own—on a bike. Everyone tried to tell her no, she couldn't do it. She was like *yes I can*. She got a job, saved up, went to the library, read all about South America and apprenticed at a bike shop to learn how to fix bikes. Then she bought a one-way ticket to Venezuela, not even knowing any Spanish. She learned Spanish by talking to people, rode her bike from country to country, lived with people she met, ignored their warnings not to go to Colombia, and even found work as a botanist's assistant in the rainforest.

Patrick Meehan was never good at school, which he hated, and in seventh grade he dropped out. The main thing Patrick liked to do was play video games. With a bright future ahead of him, he took a series of dead-end art jobs. He had never been good at math or science (and he still isn't), but he took to computer programming. By the time he was 20, he had a big time job with Nintendo designing technology for video games. I read about him in *Smithsonian* Magazine.

The self-schooling movement includes people of all ages who take their educations into their own hands. I think we're going to see the self-schooling movement grow quietly and quickly, kind of like the vegetarian movement. Ten and 20 years ago, if you were a vegetarian, everyone thought you were crazy. You couldn't eat at most restaurants because there was nothing vegetarian on the menu. And everyone knew meat was good for you—one of the four food groups you had to eat every day. Today, everyone knows that meat is bad for you and it's bad for the environment. Being vegetarian is becoming mainstream and society is changing to accommodate it. McDonalds and Burger King now have vegetarian options. Public schools will one day be forced to accommodate self-schoolers.

I'm sick of hearing supposedly concerned people say, "Schools can't be expected to fix problems that start in the home." Well homes can't fix problems that start in the school either! And how many of these so-called "home problems" are caused by previous generations of people being programmed to fail in school?

The typical white upper-class view is that the poor and black and Latino people have behavior problems and the way to help them is to sit them down at a desk and teach them to act more like us. Wait a minute. Poor black and Latino people didn't invent guns and crack and TV and cigarettes and cars and

BY CHRISTINE WONG

Air Jordans and gambling and welfare. Poor black and Latino people didn't sail over to Europe, put our asses in the bottom of a ship, destroy our way of life, enslave us, put us in ghettos and pretend it's not their fault. I think that upper-class white people have a behavior problem and the main problem with people in the ghetto is that they're trying too hard to act like us. They just don't have the resources to get away with it.

Anyone who *actually knows* any poor and black and Latino people knows that even with all the set backs they experience, a decent percentage of them could do a much better job educating their own kids than any school if they only had the basic resources, and the sense that it was possible.

Grace Llewellyn's books will give people the sense that it is possible.

Getting them the resources will be more difficult.

That's why we're starting The Self Education Foundation and an Unalumni Association so that successful people who quit school (like Liz Claiborne, Whoopie Goldberg, and Joseph LeMandt—the youngest person on the *Forbes* 400) can give "unscholarships" to self-education resource centers for low-income families whose children want to take responsibility for their own learning.

The upper-classes have always been able to hire tutors for their children. The information age and the rise of home offices is once again making it possible for middle-class parents not to send their kids to school. Maybe the energy of the middle-class unschooling movement will inspire the underclass to see their own experiences with school in a different light—to realize that bad grades don't mean they're stupid—and to take a greater interest in their children's education.

But here's the big question, How will they get jobs?

Resumés. Portfolios. Relationships. Internships. Experience. Letters of recommendation. Hello? That's how adults get jobs. Why not teenagers? Resumés allow employers a more precise screen for young applicants, not just a boilerplate diploma. Most poor kids miss these crucial career steps because they're forced to go directly from school into dead-end jobs. There's no better way to prove you can do something than by doing it.

For some reason, a lot of otherwise intelligent liberal-thinking people have a problem with this. A lot of my friends and the people I respect most in the world are teachers or work their asses off attempting to reform the public school system. Every time they hear me say the word "homeschooling," all they can think about are right-wing isolationist kooks who teach their kids civics by harassing women outside abortion clinics. And they worry rightly that if all the brightest, most self-directed, kids quit school, it will further undermine an already struggling public education system, which they are working diligently to improve.

So here's my thing. I'm not dissing public education reform. I am definitely not dissing public school teachers. Teaching five classes a day of 30 kids—shoot, their job is hard enough! And I'm not saying homeschooling is good. I'm saying that self-directed education is the essence of learning whether or not kids are in school. I'm saying wake up and smell the coffee: most public schools are not very public. They're segregated as hell, even the integrated schools have segregated tracking. Most ghetto schools are junior jails and no school reform in America is going to change that. Meanwhile, homeschooling is the fastest growing education movement in America. The right-wing uses homeschooling strategically to prepare their young to network and do research and picket abortion clinics and lobby their state representatives while our next generation is sitting in school reading from a textbook. Guess what? They're gonna kick our asses up and down the block.

We need a homeschooling movement with a political analysis. How are we going to support and connect homeschoolers across race and class? How do we help kids convince their parents to let them out of the house and into the world? How do we transmit our love of learning, of people, of justice, of action? How do we support homeschoolers to create a life for themselves that is *more* public than public school?

THAT'S FINE FOR MIDDLE-CLASS WHITE KIDS LIKE YOU, BUT MY CHILDREN NEED A HIGH-SCHOOL DIPLOMA

Some people say, "Yeah, self-education may be fine for white kids from educated backgrounds. But it's irresponsible to encourage black kids from the ghetto to dropout of school. School is the only chance they've got."

Really?

Are you *sure*—or is that the drug talking?

Llewellyn's latest book, *Freedom Challenge: African-American Homeschoolers*, features 15 essays written by black families who have taken their educations into their own hands. One black mother decided to pull her son out of school after reading the book *Countering the Conspiracy to Destroy Black Boys* by Jawanza Kunjufu:

> "When Sean was in kindergarten, I was receiving at least one call a week from his school, telling me that my five-year-old was a 'menace to society.' After getting through that year, we began to experience the disaster of the public school system. Two months into the school year, Sean's teacher informed us that Sean was going to fail the first grade and that he needed special education.... Next came Catholic school. There, I was told that Sean had Attention Deficit Disorder and we should put him on Ritalin. He was also given an IQ test and we discovered that he had one of the highest scores in the school."

It doesn't take a Ph.D. in education to see how many bright-eyed and curious black and brown and poor children who get labeled with behavior problems in pre-school end up sad and in drug-rehab twenty years down the pike.

How many times have you heard this story? "Little Johnny is a bright child but he doesn't apply himself in school." Then Little Johnny becomes Lazy Johnny, or Hyperactive Johnny, or Angry and Withdrawn Johnny, and then Bad Johnny and Suspended Johnny. Special Ed Johnny. Stupid Johnny. Drugs and Alcohol Johnny. Fuck All Y'all Johnny. Juvi Hall Johnny. No Skills to be Employed Johnny. In and Out the Joint Johnny. Deadbeat Dad Johnny. Mama's little boy Johnny, where did he go wrong?

Everyone knows the problem with Johnny is that he didn't stay in school. Everyone knows that "staying in school is good" and "dropping-out is bad." We've all heard the statistics. On average, dropouts earn only a third the income of those who graduate from college. Dropouts are many times more likely to end up incarcerated. But what if the statistics don't tell the whole story?

Carl Upchurch is an elementary school dropout *and* a college graduate. He grew up in South Philly. His apartment was the nightmare "hip spot in the neighborhood" for all the pimps, hoes, and drug slangers (his family) who barely gave a shit about him. "At school," he says. "I was constantly chastised for being who I was. I couldn't relate to it. I didn't see Dick and Jane's mother shooting heroin in her arm. My teachers saw me as a sullen child. I wasn't sullen at all. I was *tired* from being kept up all night. I was *sad*. I was *ashamed*. I was *intimidated*, but I wanted to learn. By fourth grade, I was responding to school the way most African-American males respond to school—I wasn't. Some put their heads on the desk and don't respond for another five or six years and then dropout. I just got up and left."

He was in fourth grade. Where Malcolm X had been a hustler, Carl Upchurch became a straight-out thug. He spent the next two decades beating the shit out of people, in and out of prison. The better he got at fighting, the more he gained confidence to learn other things. "When the '60s jumped off, it was fashionable to stay abreast of current events. I wanted to know 'Who was Rap Brown?' 'What was the SCLC all about?' 'What is CORE?' They were in the news every day. It was action-packed. I found out that I liked to read. Reading was this power. It gave me ammunition to dialogue with the teachers and the little unit guards. I began to question them. Then the other kids would say, 'Go on Carl, tell that mothafucka.' I got props for it. I could put 'military-industrial complex' in a sentence. I got that encouragement so I had to keep learning."

Locked in solitary one time, Upchurch found a book of Shakespeare's sonnets that was used to prop up a table leg and out of sheer boredom began to read it. To his surprise, it spoke to him. "I had been given the impression that this stuff was beyond my ability to comprehend so I stayed away from it. Now I began to realize I could learn a lot of things. I began to get serious and I realized I might have a few things to say myself. I felt I had all this knowledge and I had to wake people up. I would say, 'Go ahead, eat the cancer! You know they put pesticide on that food.' I started shouting in my cell block, having arguments out loud with the authors I was reading. I started writing letters to the newspaper and they started printing them. I wrote to Angela Davis, Huey Newton, Bobby Seale, an actress in England named Vanessa Redgrave and they wrote me back."

Eventually Upchurch got a college degree through the University of Pittsburgh. He couldn't have gotten it today—prison education programs were cut during the '80s and '90s. He organized the national gang truce summit in 1993, and wrote a book called *Convicted in the Womb*, which is being made into a movie.

There's a long tradition of black people educating themselves in prison or dropping-out of school and succeeding without a diploma: Malcolm X, August Wilson, Patti LaBelle, Whoopie Goldberg, KRS-ONE, Nas and so on. Elijah Muhammad was arrested in the 1930s for refusing to send his own kids to public school. Black families have always found secret ways to educate themselves, or they wouldn't be "free" today.

Yet homeschooling, the "H" word, has been a taboo subject for many black parents and educators. ""Historically, we fought to get into the schools, so the idea of fighting to get out of schools doesn't make sense to a lot of people," says Donna Nichols-White, publisher of *The Drinking Gourd*, a multi-cultural home-education magazine. The Drinking Gourd refers to the constellation (also called "big dipper") which Harriet Tubman followed to free slaves through the Underground Railroad. In the same way, Nichols-White sees homeschooling as a modern day freedom movement.

Homeschooling support groups, newsletters, web pages, curricula, conferences, degree programs (and also scams) are everywhere. But homeschooling has such stigma as a 'kooky white fringe thing.' that most people don't know the basic facts. The number of kids homeschooling has skyrocketed from around 20,000 in the 1970s to about a million today. It is now legal in all 50 states. Requirements vary, but most states don't even require the parent to have a high-school diploma.

Most colleges now accept homeschoolers, partly because they tend to score above average on standardized tests. Reed Colfax became famous in the late '80s as the first black person without a high-school diploma to attend Harvard University (and Yale Law School). "We didn't consider ourselves homeschoolers when we first started," says Colfax. "It was much more of a survival technique for my parents, 'We're pretty poor. We need the kids to work on the farm. The schools around here are pretty poor. Maybe we can do a better job ourselves.'"

Obviously not everyone can do it. "To homeschool, you have to have a mother or father around who cares about you," says Carl Upchurch. "But otherwise, I think it's great. I'm starting to hear about homeschooling everywhere I speak, especially from black people. Schools are still educating kids as if it's the Nineteenth Century." And with the dropout rate still 40-80% in many ghetto public schools, the question for many young people is not *whether* they'll quit school but *when*, how many years they'll waste in the meantime, and how damaged they'll be when they come out.

Joaquin Cotten is a homeschooler from East Harlem whose parents pulled him out after first grade. "No major crisis had happened," says his mother ArtyAnn Cotten. "There were just subtle things that were beginning to erode his spirit. We were already witnessing what classically happens to black males in our society. I knew we needed to do something different."

In contrast to many homeschooling families who try to recreate a school atmosphere in their homes, the Cottens helped structure their son's education around his own interests. "When Joaquin was eight, he read a biography of [the celebrated black photographer] Gordon Parks. He was fascinated by Gordon Parks," says Ms. Cotten. "Well, we found out Gordon Parks was having an exhibit in New York. Joaquin said he was going to go meet him. He was determined. He got all dressed up with his camera around his neck and a portfolio. We went with him to this gallery in Soho, and we were standing outside waiting for my husband. And there was this woman. She asked Joaquin if he was a photographer. He said "Yes". She asked to see his photos. He showed them to her. She said, "Oh, these are very nice. A good photographer always carries business cards." So he pulls out his wallet and gives her a business card. And she laughed, she said, "Oh, you have to meet my father." So she took him upstairs. We didn't know who this woman was. She turned out to be Gordon Parks' daughter, Toni Parks. She brought him to meet Gordon Parks who gave him a critique of his portfolio. Our whole approach to education is based on nurturing Joaquin's own interests, going to the source, doing the research, finding out for ourselves."

At 12 years old, Joaquin has already won the prestigious *National Geographic World* International photo contest. He has had three gallery exhibits, and his work has been reviewed by the *New York Times,* which neglected to mention he was a homeschooler. "If he hadn't been homeschooling then he wouldn't have had time to do this," says his mother. "He wouldn't have had time to spend with his father who is a great influence. Without homeschooling, this would not have been possible."

THE BLACK HOMESCHOOLING MOVEMENT

Education specialist Jawanza Kunjufu sees an increasing number of black families homeschooling. Demand for his SET CLAE curriculum for homeschoolers has grown every year since he published it in 1990.

"There are a lot of reasons to consider homeschooling," Kunjufu says. "If you videotape a class of black students in kindergarten, then you videotape them again in eighth grade, it will break your heart. Their curiosity, desire for learning, eagerness, is completely gone. People try to say there is a lack of motivation. There didn't seem to be a lack of motivation in kindergarten. Something happened to them in those eight years of school to suck the motivation out of them. They associate being smart with being white. They associate education with getting grades, not learning. School is not designed to educate. It is designed to categorize and destroy. Blacks make up seventeen percent of the school population, but forty one percent of those in Special Ed."

Homeschooling advocates are frustrated that despite well-documented problems with school, most parents still feel homeschooling is out of the question. "My children built a robot dinosaur which they can computer control,"" says Dorina Nichols-White. "I mean, it's *walking across the table* and people *still* have the nerve to ask me why I homeschool. This *[XXL]* is the first black magazine that has been willing to even talk about black homeschooling. No one else is even interested in any form of education other than school. I speak every year at the National Black Child Development Institute. This year was the first time I put in a proposal to talk about homeschooling and it was the first time my topic was rejected."

Even the idea of homeschooling is still foreign to most parents. "I keep answering the same questions over and over again," says ArtyAnn Cotten, who publishes a homeschooling newsletter for people of color *On the Backs of Our Ancestors*. "Yes, it's legal. Yes, people of color can do it. Yes, you can do it on a low budget, but you do have to be creative. Yes, I know single mothers on welfare who've done it successfully. Yes, there are Latino and Asian homeschoolers."

Long Island native Asiba Tupahache, a single mother of two, has been homeschooling since the 1970s, "I wouldn't send my children to school any more than I'd send them to Jeffrey Dahmer Daycare," she says. "School has become a normalized condition—like black eyes . . . 'that means he loves me.' The biggest damage school does to us is learning that *we can't believe our own experience*. We've been beaten up so badly that we repeatedly fail to believe we have what we've got. So I finally realized just because other people were protecting their delusions didn't mean I had to."

Tupahache is a former public school teacher. "Having been a public school teacher, I felt like I worked in the kitchen of that restaurant. I knew what was going on. I even taught at a Native school and it was the same bullshit with feathers painted on the outside. It took me years to work through that. There are issues of addiction involved. My kids understand things now that I never understood until I was in my 30s. My 15-year-old daughter speaks Japanese and can write in three different script structures. Do you hear me? *Three script structures of Japanese.* It never would've *occurred* to me to study Japanese on my own. I didn't feel inner-permission to learn anything on my own. I didn't teach it to her. Homeschooling is not about me being her only teacher. Homeschooling is about learning from everyone, from the janitor, from the woman behind the meat counter. Homeschooling is a mislabeling of what is in reality world learning."

Call it what you like, most parents feel homeschooling is impossible because they work. "Homeschooling is the best thing since sliced bread," says rapper Ras Kass. "If your own mama won't teach you, then who will? But realistically, a lot of families can't afford to do that." Even Asiba Tupahache sent her kids to school for a few years when she had no other choice.

Most low-income homeschooling parents had to struggle to find a way. Maurci Jackson is a single mother from Chicago who founded United Parents Against Lead (UPAL), and homeschools her two daughters while traveling around the country, crusading against lead poisoning. "It's all about your priorities," says Zakia Shabazz, head of UPAL Virginia. "My husband and I retired and we cut back on a lot of things we had indulged in and didn't need anyway. We put the more important things first. The cost of homeschooling is as low as public school because we don't have to buy any of these fancy school clothes. We don't have to pack a separate lunch or pay for transportation. And we get a lot of books donated to us surplus. We form co-ops, take turns and do it in rotation. I bake bean pies and my husband sells them."

The emerging information economy and the rocketing popularity of homeschooling internationally (even in Japan), are forcing parents who considered homeschooling crazy a few years ago to take a second look. The job market is changing. More people are working out of their homes. Workers need to be more independent and entrepreneurial, to network, to communicate across cultures, and to continue learning life-long.

"We've been through higher education. We know the value, but we also know the pitfalls," says Paula Penn-Nabrit. She and her husband Charles Nabrit own their own management consulting business and live in the suburbs of Columbus, Ohio, where they were spending $20,000 a year to send three sons to an elite prep school with no black teachers. When they became insistent about the need to hire black teachers, the school found an excuse to kick their sons out.

"It was a blessing in disguise. We began to ask ourselves, 'Is this really the kind of place we want to send our children? Maybe we don't need to spend our money and energy telling white people what to do. Maybe we need to spend it on ourselves."

"We believe in holistic learning—intellectual, physical and spiritual. We are Pentecostal Apostolic Christians and we want our sons to know that spiritual growth and intellectual growth are not mutually exclusive. We also want discipline. School goes all year. They don't get summers off. We are preparing them for real life and in real life you don't get summers off. We have a mandatory reading period of two hours per day. Some parents says it's cruel to make your kids sit and read for two hours a day. But some of the same parents will have their kids sit for six hours to get their hair braided."

Every Monday, the family reads the *New York Times* Week in Review and they argue about it. "They're expected to know what's going on in the world," says Penn-Nabrit. "It's not enough to only read people you agree with. And that leads nicely into the study of World Religions. They are familiar with Judaism, Hindu scriptures, and the Qu'ran. As well as traditional philosophers, Plato, Aristotle, Kant, they read Steven Biko, Derrick Bell, Malcolm X, Dr. King, Frederick Douglass. For history, we began with Africa, where civilization started, and then followed the natural migration of peoples to Asia, Europe, and the Americas. We got textbooks from Ohio State University and we hired African and African-American male tutors to teach them math and foreign languages. The results are remarkable."

For science, all three sons have volunteered 2000 hours—each—at the science museum downtown. "And they played football on a team in what you'd call a classic inner-city area. Most importantly, they get to spend a lot of time with their father who they are very close to." The oldest sons have both scored exceptionally high on the SATs and are expecting to attend Ivy League colleges (they both chose Princeton).

The biggest question homeschooling parents get is socialization. "People ask me 'how can your child survive without being socialized in their belief system?'" says Asiba Tupahache. "It's as if people think socialization is only possible in a school institution and that this type of socialization is remotely desirable, let alone necessary. It's difficult for some of us to think of doing for self. Some of us are very dependent on government agencies and bureaucracies and find it hard to believe we can do anything without permission. Why do you think homeschooled kids always do so well in college? They already know how to seek out what they need. So many school kids act like they're breaking free from prison when they get to college. Homeschool kids are already oriented to developing a true thirst for learning, not cheating on an exam so they can pass. People talk about taking a vacation. Vacation from what? We're living and learning all the time. School systems can seem like the only safe place for some of our youth whose homes are very problematic. What seems to escape us is that we are our own answers. We get a lot of calls about homeschooling from parents who are in crisis. A teacher has already abused your kid or they're being put into special ed or welfare is coming to take your kids away. We try to tell parents, 'Don't wait for a crisis to consider homeschooling'."

Wise Intelligent of the rap group PRT (Poor Righteous Teachers) dropped-out of school when he was 15. "Public school was not working. I used to be an 'A' student, but ever since second grade, I hated school. I used to hide my shoes before school so I wouldn't have to go. When I would come to school, I was chaos. I *stayed* in the office. I *stayed* in in-school suspension. I started selling weed. Robbing heads for their weed. Doing so many foul things I'm not proud of and I don't know why brothers choose to glorify on their records. School was just a hang out. It was like going to the club, smoking weed, trippin', talking to girls, getting into fights. Everybody's numb. They ain't feelin nothin. I started learning just for spite. That's what made me who I am today. I was the poor kid. I didn't have nothing. I educated myself. In 8th grade, I became a Five Percenter. My crew, we would challenge the teachers. We would find ways to debate anything. My history teacher caught a bad one daily. When I was 14, I read *The Autobiography of Malcolm X.* I stole it out of the school library. I would just read and read and read. Everywhere PRT goes, Shaheed goes into record stores, I go into bookstores. I'm digging in the crates too, not for records, but for books."

Hip-hop has always been about self-directed learning. Crazy Legs didn't become a b-boy in gym class. Phase 2 didn't create softie letters (a.k.a. "bubble letters") in Art History. Grandmaster Flash didn't invent the cross-fader by getting a degree in electrical engineering. Grandmaster Caz didn't learn to MC in English class. And Russell Simmons didn't need an MBA to start Def Jam. Homeschooling is about learning every subject the way we learn hip-hop.

"I think homeschooling is the best way," says Wise Intelligent. "I'm not saying school is all bad; you can learn anywhere, but if I had been homeschooled, I would probably be an archeologist right now. I would be in Egypt. I would be all over the world, analyzing evidence from tombs and setting history straight."

Homeschools sometimes grow into larger schools. The Shabazz family lives in a low-income area surrounded by projects on the South Side of Richmond, Virginia. "Everyone commented on how well-behaved and well-spoken the children were," said Zakia Shabazz. "The school system was astonished at how high they were testing." Within two years, the Shabazz family found themselves homeschooling a total of 18 children from nine neighborhood families. This fall, they are starting Shabazz Academy, a small, affordable private school with a homeschool feel.

"When we started the African People's Action School in Trenton in 1976, we began with four children and two teachers," says Mwalimu Shujaa. Shujaa is author of *Too Much Schooling, Too Little Education,* and Executive Officer of the Council of Independent Black Institutions (CIBI), a network of fifty afrocentric schools across the country. "It could be said that we were homeschooling in a sense, but then other people sent their children and we created an institution. Businesses grew out of that, and village-like relationships with professionals and entrepreneurs supporting each other and bartering services. That could be one limitation of homeschooling for some families, the isolation from other people with similar commitments. We're beginning to see many homeschooling families contacting our schools."

There are a couple of informal black homeschooling networks taking shape. The Seeds of Many Nations Collective was founded by three women from the New York Area, Asiba Tupahache, ArtyAnn Cotten, Francis Poe in Brooklyn, and from Michigan, Kristin Cleage Williams who started one of the first black homeschooling newsletters *Umoja-Unidad-Unity* which is now

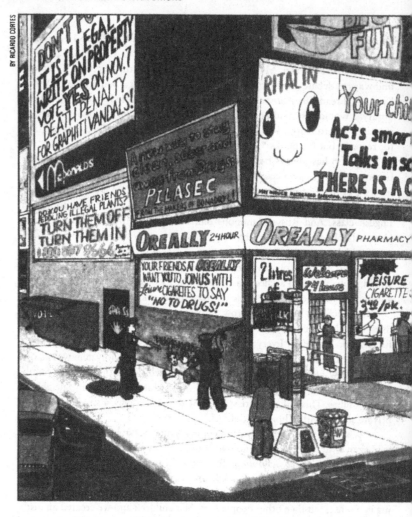

known as *African-American Resources* on-line. They organized The Leothy Miller Owens Homeschool Conference in Brooklyn last year which explored, among other things, the connection between homeschooling and prison self-education. As a featured speaker, they invited Eddie Ellis, a former Black Panther in prison for 23 years, who educated himself as part of a prison think-tank. Ellis now runs the Community Justice Center in Harlem.

It seems that homeschooling, hip-hop and prison study are three forms of self-education that have a lot to learn from each other. The problem with homeschooling is that it's too white, too sheltered and too boring. The problem with hip-hop is that it's too narrow-minded, too commercial and too

superficial. The problem with prison study is that it's too late.

Homeschooling isn't a solution to every problem and there's no guarantee that every family can make it work. But everyone who's done it seems to swear by it. "I think every kid should be exposed to homeschooling," says Sunshine Lewis of Pensacola, Florida who recently enrolled in a junior college. It is her first time in school. She is 15 and plans to finish college by the time she's 19 so she can get on to other things. "Most people think it's wonderful that I'm home-schooling but they say 'I could never do that.' People think even if it would work, they don't have the time and they don't have the confidence to do it. One question a lot of people don't ask is, 'How much worse could it be?'"

A GOURMET GUIDE TO SELF-EDUCATION

So you're thinking of going back to school to continue your education?

Let me save you $50,000.

People always say that—at its best—school teaches you how to think, how to learn. But what kind of thinking and learning did it teach?

Here are 19 strategies that have worked for me and other self-schoolers. Use them as they apply. You won't be tested and you won't be graded on how well you use them in your life. The hardest part of self-education is that there are no external rewards or structures—you must accept the responsibility that you are the student, the principal, and the superintendent. If your self-education doesn't work out, there's no one else to blame.

1. You _are_ self-motivated. "But I'm not self-motivated . . . " Oh, really? Then why are you reading this book? "I'm reading it for fun." Exactly.

2. You're allowed to have fun. From dance to math, sex to stock picking, fixing your car to fighting suburban sprawl, give yourself permission to have fun while learning whatever you damn well please in whatever way you please it. The point of self-education is not to continue the feelings of inadequacy you picked up in school.

3. Learn with friends. Self-education doesn't necessarily mean _by yourself._ The most important part is finding the right teachers who will support you and push you if necessary to learn what you want. If it gets too comfortable learning with your friends, then ask yourself whether you're really getting to the good stuff.

4. Scare away your shyness. I was a painfully shy child. In sixth grade, I convinced my parents to let me transfer to a mostly black public school which I was terrified of. I'm not shy anymore. Black people saved me.

5. Save all your ideas. Don't assume you will remember the good ones. I write all mine down. I carry a notebook with me at all times—a small notebook I retire quickly because I'm prone to losing them. I jot down every idea I get and I put a star next to the ones I want to keep. My "idea file" has 300 entries and I tape it to my wall so I can update it regularly.

6. Create your own curriculum. My "reading list" is 12 pages long—every book anyone recommends to me, organized by category. If a book comes up three times, it goes to the top of the list. But with any great book, be sure to read the critiques so you don't become a crackpot.

7. Act on what you learn. I know it's a weird concept if you've spent your life in school. But if you don't change your life in some way every time you learn something, then what did you really learn? You need to set up mechanisms to change habits, and you need to keep setting yourself challenges to reach for. People think I'm torturing myself by waking up at 4 AM to go jogging before rush hour. No! It brings me *joy*.

8. Questions questions questions. Are you asking enough questions? Are you asking what you *really* want to know? And are you asking follow-up questions "Why?" "How?" "How do you know?" "Really?"—or do you start talking again as soon as they answer your first one?

9. Conferences conferences conferences. Whatever you're into, there are conferences for it. You'll find them advertised in magazines or on the Internet. Go to them. Last year, I went to seven conferences in seven months: The Prairie Festival in Kansas; a youth of color leadership summit at Vassar College, the Saguaro Group on civic engagement at Harvard, a philanthropy conference in Seattle, the National Organizers Alliance community organizing retreat in Colorado, and the Media and Democracy Congress in New York. I was a counselor in Oregon at Not Back To School Camp, a camp run by *Teenage Liberation Handbook* author Grace Llewellyn. The whole thing cost me less than $1600, including travel, which may sound like a lot until you compare it to the price of attending college, owning a car, or a lot of other things people believe it is necessary to spend their money on. Love conferences. Talk to everyone. Meet your heroes. Get disillusioned. Meet amazing people no one is listening to. Get inspired. Get their numbers. Draft them as your mentors.

10. Feed and water your mentors. Most people—even famous and renowned people—feel under-appreciated. If you like someone for a specific reason, tell them tell them tell them. You'll be surprised to learn how few people ever do. Tell them specifically what you want to learn from them, at their convenience, and how helping you learn this will further their ultimate goals. I have more than three dozen mentors on my mentor list. And I keep a much bigger list of people who I want to be my mentors.

11. Lists are good—indispensable for the self-structured learner. They do not mean you're a control freak. A friend of mine used to hate lists and "list makers," until I made her a list of all the things I love about her. She doesn't hate lists anymore.

12. Long and short-term goal setting. I have written down 50-year, five-year, three-, two- and one-year goals as well as monthly, weekly, and daily "to do" lists. I make them because I need them. Not everyone does.

13. I never feel guilty that I don't do a fraction of what's on any of my lists—their function is to remind, to preserve, to let me see patterns, inspire new combinations, keep my mind off petty shit and celebrate the possibilities.

14. You don't have to quit school to self-school. I'm proud of you if you can sit through school. But don't think it's an education. Never sign up for classes based on course descriptions. Before you sign up for any class, spend an afternoon on campus and survey at least fifty students to see who their favorite teachers are. See which names come up over and over again. Sit in on classes to see which ones you really like, *then* decide which classes to take. Also, remember that it's less important to get good grades than to network with your classmates—the future grassroots leaders, CEOs and anyone else who interests you. Get a foundation of down-to-earth friends who will hold you accountable. Do what you need to do to make yourself happy so you don't become burnt-out. Then get power—get that MBA, that JD. Those on the outside need allies inside the system.

15. Celebrate what you learn. Since I never graduated college, there was no sense of closure, so now, at age 25, I'm throwing myself a college "self-graduation" ceremony to share my education with my family and friends. I recently went to a bat-mitzvah and an African-American rites-of-passage ceremony. They gave me lots of ideas to invent my own ceremony.

16. Friendship is learning. Especially when you're building friendships with people you find intimidating or awkward to deal with. Even people you thought you could never be friends with: your hated parents and siblings, cold-faced men in suits, independent-minded women, angry teenagers, shy cousins, bosses, employees, whiny children, activists, new-agers, religious fundamentalists, gays, celebrities, criminals, invalids, foreigners, poor people, rich people, the aloof, the overly gregarious, the depressed, the egotistical, the needy, the manipulative and the self-deluded. Learning to become friends with more kinds of people and bringing out the best in each other is the core of any self-education.

17. Learning is scary. Learning sounds so nice and innocent, doesn't it? Tell that to Adam and Eve! Learning is *scary*. It's okay to be scared, and you should be. The better you get at learning, the more you'll be required to change the basic assumptions of your life. And the more you'll be forced to confront that the way you were living before was backwards as hell. I know it's tempting to feel that you already have everything figured out. But the truth is, you're just as dumb as the rest of us. What did you think? God swooped down and personally hand-picked you to be smarter than everyone else? And even if you are smarter, that just means you have to fight twice as hard not to rest on your laurels.

18. Beware of teaching. When you start teaching more than you're learning, it means you're falling off. For example, in the time it took me to write this article, I could have read two or three books. Our relationship is unfair now because you're learning something from me (I hope) and I still haven't learned anything from you. So now you can return the favor. I'm starting a Self-Education Foundation that will make it possible for more young people, especially poor kids from difficult environments—like my old hero KRS-

One—to educate themselves outside of school. To start this organization, I am looking for names of highly successful high-school or college dropouts, individual donors with an interest in self-education, and enthusiastic volunteers. So if you learned anything from me, please take a minute to think if you know of anyone in the above categories whom you'd recommend for the board, donor, or volunteer base of the Self-Education Foundation. Please send names and contact info to: The Self Education Foundation, P.O. Box 30790, Philadelphia, PA, 19104.

19. Never be too proud to ask for help!

THE SELF-EDUCATION FOUNDATION

I received more than 500 letters and emails when the above article originally appeared in Utne Reader. (I was just learning to use e-mail and I lost about 300 e-mails before I was able to reply.)

However, I am proud to report that The Self-Education Foundation is off the ground. It is run by myself and three kick-ass young homeschoolers, Karl T. Muth from Chicago (17), Emily Nepon from Philadelphia (21), and Adriyel Paymer from Atlanta (20). We have a newsletter, a web site (www.selfeducation.org.), email that works (info@selfeducation.org.) And we have already made our first round of 12 small grants to grassroots self-education organizations, many of which are listed below. And we have a fiscal sponsor through which we accept tax-deductible contributions.

Self-Education Resources

- *On the Backs of Our Ancestors* people of color homeschooling newsletter P.O. Box 1058, NY, NY, 10028. $15/yr. seednews@aol.com
- *The Drinking Gourd,* multi-cultural home-education magazine and catalog P.O. Box 2557, Redmond, WA, 98073. $15/yr. (800)TDG-5487
- *African-American Resources* homeschooling newsletter (formerly *Umoja-Unidad-Unity)* Kriswms@aol.com 5621 S. Lakeshore Dr., Idlewild, MI, 49642.
- *As for Me and My House* by Paula Penn-Nabrit, P.O. Box 1174, Westerville, OH, 43086-1174
- SETCLAE curriculum by Jawanza Kunjufu, African-American Images, 1909 W. 95th St., Chicago, IL, 60643. (800)552-1991.
- Council of Independent Black Institutions P.O. Box 1327, Buffalo, NY, 14215.

- Growing Without Schooling, Holt Associates, 2269 Mass Ave., Cambridge, MA, 02140.
- Alternative Education Resource Organization, 417 Roslyn Rd., Roslyn Hts., NY, 11577.
- *Teenage Liberation Handbook: How to Quit School and Get a Real Life and Education* ($17.95); *Real Lives: Eleven Teenagers Who Don't Go to School* ($17.95); *Freedom Challenge: African-American Homeschoolers* ($19.95) by Grace Llewellyn, Lowry House, (503) 686-2315, P.O. Box 1014, Eugene, OR, 97440. (prices include post).

URBAN LIFE VS. SUBURBAN SPRAWL

WHY I LOVE MY NEIGHBORHOOD

I was thinking about that TV show Mister Rogers' Neighborhood and how alien a concept it has become to "know the people in your neighborhood." These days, most people don't even know who lives on their block.

The more time I spend in the suburbs, subdivisions and strip malls of America, the more I have come to appreciate the place I grew up. It's called Hyde Park, an affluent university neighborhood on the South Side of Chicago. I spent a lot of *Bomb the Suburbs* saying how hypocritical Hyde Park is, but there's a lot I took for granted growing up there that I am only now beginning to realize most Americans never get a chance to enjoy.

For example, within three blocks of my apartment, there are four bus lines, one train line, a world-class museum, two huge parks, a little park, a public housing project for disabled people, a fancy restaurant and a dollar store, a stock broker and a check-cashing place. (In Chicago, we call them "currency exchanges" even though they don't exchange foreign currency.) We have a neighborhood dive bar and a flower store, a Mexican restaurant, three Thai restaurants, two Middle-Eastern restaurants, a Japanese restaurant, a Korean restaurant, two Palestinian-owned grocery stores, a black-owned grocery store and two that I'm not sure who owns. There are a black-owned coffee shop, a black-owned car repair, five black-owned beauty salons and there used to be a black-owned video store until it was crushed by the chains. Altogether, we probably have five times as many locally-owned businesses as chain stores. There is an electronics repair shop, a bike shop, a shoe repair, believe it or not, a *butcher.* And, oh yeah, a lake. All within a short walk of my spot.

I took all of this for granted. In most parts of the country, people have little reason to walk anymore.

I took for granted that on my block are houses that cost half a million dollars, and low-income apartments. Ninety percent of the housing in my neighborhood is at least 50 years old. My apartment was built in 1913. It has big old trees out back that are taller than the building itself, beautiful details carved into the facade, and lion faces guarding the roof. All the old buildings in my neighborhood are beautiful. You could spend hours just looking at the details on the buildings on my block. Our local grocery store is a co-op which my parents are members of. Our local bookstore is a co-op which my parents are members of. We have used bookstores. The most popular restaurant in the neighborhood, The Medici, has graffiti all over the walls. They sponsor tons of local, community events and efforts. When I was 13-years-old, the owner of The Medici, Hans Morsbach, took a chance and paid me more than $300 to paint a graffiti mural on the inside of the restaurant. When I was 14, he paid me and my friend $500 to paint the side of one of his other restaurants.

Try walking a plan like that into your local Red Lobster.

At the time, I took it for granted. Now I see just how rare it is. When people ask me what my goals are in life, one of them is to make more American communities a little bit more like Hyde Park—racially, economically and socially.

But like I said, Hyde Park isn't all good.

How the Good People of Hyde Park are Sucking the Life Out of Urban Childhood

THE BASKETBALL KIDNAPPINGS

"Hyde Park basketball courts had remained stubbornly black as areas around them whitened and went upscale . . . .The courts were under suspicion and the older players knew it. But discretion was of no avail. The courts were being swept away. The first to go was the most perfect court known to man. It was situated among the trees just off Lake Shore Drive, its eastern basket facing the lake. Gliding to that basket, with lake and sky beyond gave you the illusion of flight. The second court to disappear was less beautiful but much loved by its players . . . .Shortly before the annual tournament, the backboards were taken down and carted away under cover of darkness."

—Brent Staples, *Parallel Time*

That was in the 1970s.

There are now no public basketball hoops in Hyde Park.

Last summer, I was walking down an alley off 55th Street. A white father and two boys were playing basketball inside a gated yard.

In a parking lot across the alley sat six black boys of comparable age, noticeably sullen.

I went over to the black boys. "Why don't you play?"

"They won't let us."

"Did you ask?"

"Yeah. They said no. Will you ask for us?"

Will I ask for you? Oh . . . I'm white too.

"Excuse me. I was wondering if there's any chance we could pl—"

"No. Sorry. This is our yard. This is private property," the father said.

I walked back over to the black boys and shrugged.

"This is private property," one of them repeated.

"Dang," said the youngest. "If I had a court, I'd let them play."

"I wouldn't," said another. "'Cause they don't let us play. We should build our own hoop so when they come, we can say *no, you can't play*."

They sometimes used a hoop they made by nailing a milk crate to an electric pole in the alley. "There's too much glass in the alley," one said. I looked at the alley. It was *covered* with glass; the pavement was more pock than pave. And the building manager takes their hoop down. The boys have tried nailing their milk crates up in two other alleys but each time the hoops were mysteriously torn down the same night.

"What's your name," the oldest of the boys said to me, scowling.

He shook my hand and introduced himself as Shawn, surprising me with friendliness. "People are going to get ruthless around here in summer if there's no hoops," he said. "Black kids have nothing to do in this neighborhood. That's how they get into trouble. The only other courts are at the neighborhood club and you have to pay to become a member. Then at 47th and 43rd . . . .All the other ones have been torn down. They tried to say it was gang activity . . . .Basketball is what keeps people *out* of trouble—I *know*, I used to be in all kinds of trouble."

Chimed in the youngest, "They need to put up a whole bunch of courts and spread them around so everyone won't be crowded onto one court."

The only place on my block kids could play basketball was outside Alex O'Hara's building because his parents owned the apartment. Ms. O'Hara has to fight the neighbors just to keep her kids' milk crate up. (When she told me the names of the neighbors, they were two Hyde Park liberal families whose own kids used to play in the alley with me.) Every day in the summer, twenty kids were out there playing. Ms. O'Hara supplied popsicles and took them in if they needed a place to stay. Now even the O'Hara's milk crate is gone.

"It's very sad," said a woman who has lived on the block for 35 years. "All the kids used to play in the alley. Now they're all upstairs with computers. The kids lives today are all programmed. You look at the alley today, there's not a kid playing."

"What"s the most fun you guys have on the block?" I asked a racially mixed group of four boys whose parents have just purchased them a portable basketball hoop.

"Three summers ago, we had so much fun. We used to play kickball in the alley every night, and basketball and baseball."

It's as if the only way to have fun is to play sports.

When I was a kid growing up, way back in the '80s, sports weren't the only thing for kids in Hyde Park to do. On my block, we had:

Trees to climb and rooftops on which to build clubhouses.

WARNING

TARGET: YUPPIES

THIS BLOCK HAS BEEN SURVEYED AND CONDEMNED AS TERMINALLY INFESTED AS OF DATE:_____

To report additional problems call 312-744-5000
24 hours every day   TDD 312-744-8599

WE NEED YOUR HELP TO ELIMINATE THE YUPPIE PROBLEM IN THIS AREA.

STOP FEEDING THE YUPPIES

*YUPPIES are dangerous and healthy, mixed-income neighborhoods are their primary source of food

PROTECT YOUR FAMILY AND NEIGHBORHOOD FROM YUPPIES

*DONT support conspicuous consumption and vacuous capitalist enterprises.

*Guard your neighborhood from greedy real estate developers.

IF YUPPIES CAN'T FEED, YUPPIES CAN'T BREED

City of Chicago
Richard M. Daley
Mayor

Department of Streets
and Sanitation
Bureau of Yuppie Control

BY MICAH BAZANT

Basements to break into and hallways to steal light bulbs from.

Snowballs to throw at passing cars and at each other.

Cars to skitch in the wintertime and delivery trucks to ride.

Gangways, alleys, and yards to play all-block tag in.

Garbage chutes to slide down.

Mulberry trees and grape vines to eat off.

Tourists at the Museum of Science and Industry to mess with.

Drunks to play tricks on.

Other kids to meet and play with just walking around.

Other neighborhoods to walk to—to see what would happen.

Water to squirt, mud to make mud castles, warm tar to have tar fights.

Pedestrians to sell lemonade to.

Junk and garbage to build things out of.

Bugs, alley cats, squirrels, and birds to play with.

Lobbies to read people's magazines in.

Sports fell near the bottom of the list.

Who needed toys? We had *imaginations*. We had a *neighborhood*.

The tar pit was replaced by a parking lot. Mulberry trees and vines got cut. Our rooftop clubhouses got barb-wired. Abandoned garages were razed, gangways sealed, fences erected, and buzzer systems switched to outer doors of lobbies. The museum charges admission now, and the block next to ours is gated off. *The block next to ours is a gated community!* You have to have a special key card just to walk down what used to be a public sidewalk. I used to play in their park. Now, I have to go all the way around the block and hop a fence. They call it urban renewal. I call it nailing shut the window of communication between urban kids and adults, rich and poor, whites and blacks. The city that created people like me doesn't exist anymore.

Fifty years ago in my neighborhood, before there was air conditioning, families used to sleep outside in the park on summer nights. Twenty-five years ago, my parents met while watching the African drummers at the park by the lake. Now it's illegal to play instruments there because of complaints from residents living in high-rises more than a block away. If the people who make the rules in Hyde Park had had their way a few years earlier, my parents never would have met and I never would have been born.

No wonder I grew up feeling like the people who called the shots in my neighborhood didn't care about me.

They don't.

And they definitely didn't care about the black kids.

No wonder we wanted to write graffiti and break windows.

It's bad enough they're building more tollways and gated communities in the cornfields, sucking away resources, jobs and transit from existing communities—including present-day suburbs. But even in the city, suburb-inspired zoning has made it illegal to build alleys and "mixed-use" buildings with apartments located above storefronts. Why do you think there's a shortage of moderately priced housing? It all used to be in alleys and above storefronts! That's part of why we have a housing crisis in this country! And when did restaurants, movies, sports and cultural events become the essence of urban social life?

Ten years from now, demographics predict there'll be more middle-agers and teenagers in the population which means my block is going to be even more alienated. It's gonna take a couple more Kathy O'Haras to keep my block from getting a lot worse.

I have something for you to do this summer. Get to know the kids on your block. Invite them into your house before they invite themselves in. Find out what they need before they take it from you.

In Hyde Park, to begin with, kids need basketball courts.

SUBURBAN PLANNING

When I wrote Bomb the Suburbs, I knew little about the suburbs. By putting out the book, I received a substantial education. Random strangers would correct me on the street. "The issue isn't cities versus suburbs," said a balding white guy on an L platform, whom I was attempting to sell the book to.

"Not only Chicago, but 60 of its inner-ring or older suburbs are experiencing the same problems as Chicago: Flight of capital, flight of population, eroding tax base, rising street crime, while the outer-ring suburbs are getting subsidized to expand into the countryside—which is making the people out there furious. They don't want their wetlands paved over by tollways! That's your majority coalition that can fight these developers and this insane outward expansion of suburbia at everyone else's expense. The tollways are the linchpin of disinvestment from the city and inner-ring suburbs. A lot of groups are opposing it for different reasons, but no one sees the big picture. No one has formed a coalition to fight it and to fight for reinvestment in existing communities. You have to realize who your potential allies are and frame the issue to your advantage. Cities by themselves politically can only lose."

I think that's what he said.

He was drawing all these connections, most of which were over my head. It turned out the guy was Bob Heuer, a journalist who reported on real estate and regional issues for six years with *Crain's Chicago Business*. Finally, he got so upset by what he was learning as a reporter that he want to work applying his knowledge as an advocate fighting the tollway and suburban sprawl, trying to help bring together the majority coalition who don't yet realize we're getting screwed.

One day I went with him and some activists from one of the poorest communities in Chicago, North Lawndale, out to the Tollway Board headquarters. It was a huge glass building that looks, in Heuer's words, like "the movie set for intergalactic enterprises." All white men on the board. No minorities, no women. I realized as I was watching these people that they probably have more power over Chicago's future than Mayor Daley and no one even knows who they are. Shouldn't I have known this before I wrote the book?

An Interview with David Rusk

CITIES AND SUBURBS UNITE!

I just finished reading a book called Cities Without Suburbs, one of the best— most original, most useful—analyses of urban problems I've read. There are so many layers, I was trying to think how I'd explain it quickly. So I interviewed the author, David Rusk, the former mayor of Albuquerque, New Mexico, and an outspoken proponent of city-suburb "regionalism" and cooperation.

How would you explain your work to people who don't know anything about it?

Rusk: The question for cities has been how to defend yourself in the face of suburban sprawl. What I found when I analyzed all 320 metropolitan regions in the United States is that cities which aggressively annex their suburbs, or form consolidated city-county governments—what I call "elastic" cities like Indianapolis, Houston, Charlotte, Nashville—thrive. Cities that can't expand—"inelastic" cities like Hartford, Detroit, Cleveland, Philadelphia— pay a heavy price in concentration of poverty, segregation, a shrinking tax base and ability to attract middle-class families and businesses. Inelastic cities become regional poorhouses that act as a sinkhole to drag the entire region down, including the suburbs.

When people think of racially integrated cities, you think of New York City, San Francisco, L.A....

You have to place these cities in the context of their entire regions. The segregation index [a standard measure of racial integration for housing and schools] for blacks in the New York City region is 82 on a scale where 100 is total apartheid. The segregation index for the San Francisco region is 64. The L.A. region is 73, whereas the national average is 58. Metro Raleigh-Durham is 48. Metro Albuquerque is 39.

Why is that, other than that they're smaller and have smaller black populations?

Smaller doesn't matter. If you take York, Pennsylvania and Albuquerque, both communities are less than 3% black. York's segregation index is 71, much, much higher. The York region has 340,000 people spread over 72 municipalities and 16 school systems. Contrast York to Albuquerque, which has 500,000 people under one big municipality and one school system. Albuquerque's large, unifying public institutions spread out urban burdens and share growth benefits regionally. Our public housing is scattered over every neighborhood in a 150-square-mile city. York's public housing projects are all in a five-square-mile city. Albuquerque's not perfect. Some neighborhoods are poorer than others, but there aren't mass concentrations of poverty. And you can deal with problems on a regional level. How are you going to deal with sprawl in a place like York, where the governmental structure is so fragmented? You can, but it's tough. You have to try to get 72 municipalities to act as one.

So why haven't I heard more about these ideas?

It's not a matter of ideas or philosophy. In urban America, there are twice as many poor whites as poor blacks. But three out of four poor whites don't live in poor neighborhoods. They live in working class or middle-class neighborhoods, often in the suburbs. Two out of three poor Hispanics and three out of four poor blacks live in poor neighborhoods. But poverty in America is not like in the Third World. Only four percent of our population is both black and poor. So I say to people, "You're telling me you feel frightened and burdened by people who are four out of 100? Come on!" Most poor whites are allowed into the mainstream. They live with and go to school with middle-class kids. Most poor blacks and Hispanics have to live at critical mass . . .

Critical mass? What do you mean?

Let's use an analogy from physics. We all live with a certain level of stress which generates a low level of radioactivity. Things can happen which temporarily increase our stress level, increase our radioactivity—getting fired, divorce, a death in the family. Nothing creates more sustained stress in a person's life than poverty. If you're poor and white, you're very likely to live in a low-stress environment. You only have to deal with the stress in your own house. If you're poor and black you have to deal with your neighbors' stress as well as your own and that leads to critical mass, a social meltdown—increased crime, violence, substance abuse . . . As a former civil rights worker, I cheered as black mayors were elected across the country. But most were becoming captains of sinking ships. When you're the mayor of Camden or Detroit or Gary, Indiana, you can't really help the people who put you in office. You have to broaden the game beyond the city limits.

One criticism is regionalism dilutes black and Latino votes.

That dilution happens anyway. I did a retreat for the Richmond City Council, which has had a black majority for 20 years. Eighty percent of middle-class blacks used to live in the city. Now it's 40%. The very people a black city government counts on are leaving. In Chicago, there are in excess of 400 census tracts which are majority black. Of those, 25 have a median family income at or above the regional average. That means if you're black and you live in Chicago, you have a 95% chance of living in a community whose income is below the national average. A lot of things flow from that. You're drawing on a tax base which is below the regional average. Funding for your school district is below the regional average. It's likely that crime rates are above the regional average. So talk to me about the values of black nationalism in that context. In the realities of American society, integration works, segregation doesn't.

Who usually invites you to speak, metropolitan councils or . . .

No. Metro governments almost never exist! The largest groups are business groups, universities, city and municipal leagues and most recently church-based groups. One group to follow is the Gamaliel Foundation, which has church-based movements in 17 cities, mainly in the Midwest. They've been fighting neighborhood decline for years and realizing that even when they win, they lose. They look up and they've had all these victories and things are getting worse. Now they're trying to add an outside game—regional strategies—to their inside strategy.

What about empowerment zones?

The Baltimore empowerment zone is projected to create 8800 new jobs over a ten-year period. That's less than the number of jobs created in Baltimore's suburbs every four months! The best way to empower people is to let them move out to where the jobs are. Obviously it's more complicated than that. There are barriers of skills and education, employment networks, et cetera. The empowerment zone targets a community of 73,000 residents with a 40% poverty rate. A hundred million dollars in federal grants sounds like a lot of money, but it comes out to about $300 per year per resident. In suburban Columbia, Maryland, which has a 4% poverty rate, the federal mortgage interest deduction is worth about $300 per resident per year. Our basic policies are skewed in favor of sprawl, suburbanization, and disinvestment from older communities.

How well is regionalism catching on?

Things we were saying three or four years ago are becoming more widely embraced, but major reforms take time. The Twin Cities revenue-sharing law took four years to get enacted and another four years to get through the Supreme Court. Sprawl, poverty and race are the toughest political issues in American society. I don't see any sudden breakthroughs. Sustained change will require a grassroots movement like the civil-rights movement or the environmental movement. There are going to be winners and losers. There are 320 metropolitan regions in the country, and the ones that get their act together are going to win.

You should talk to Myron Orfield in the Twin Cities.   (1997)

An Interview with Minnesota State Representative Myron Orfield

*A CITY-SUBURB COALITION?**

I don't usually get excited about politicians. I'm excited about Myron Orfield. He's a scholar-politician, state legislator from Minneapolis and the best example I've seen of someone using a public office to vigorously promote the common good. He has managed to take issues that sounded to me and most other people like boring technical stuff—"land-use reform," "exclusive zoning," and "tax-base disparities"—and shown clearly with full-color maps why they're the real issues people should be yelling and screaming about on Jerry Springer.

These boring issues go straight to the heart of unboring issues like, "Why do we have ghettos?" "Why aren't people getting out of poverty?" "Why are Americans so scared and alienated?" and "Why are we wasting all this money paving over the countryside to build more strip malls and subdivisions?" As Orfield puts it, "Why are we throwing away one set of cities every generation to build new ones on the outer fringe?" and "Why are developers and exclusive suburbs receiving huge government tax breaks and subsidies to do it?"

Orfield has built what many thought was an impossible coalition. He has united city and suburbs, people who didn't talk to each other, didn't think they had anything in common. Business and church groups; inner-city advocates; farmers; environmentalists; and suburban homeowners and their state representatives now form a bi-partisan majority on many issues in the State Legislature. A lot of the strongest advocates for metropolitanism are now people who were against it or didn't understand it at first. Orfield was patient. He did his research, and one by one he made them see the bigger metropolitan patterns affecting their city, suburb or town—that all of us indirectly, and most of us directly, are getting screwed.

As you mentioned in your Metropolitics *book, most people still don't see why they should give a damn about metro-wide issues. How did you become aware of metro-wide issues? What was the evolution in your thinking?*

Orfield: Well, I grew up in the district I was elected in. I spent most of my life there. I was gone for most of the '80s, at Princeton and the University of Chicago. I had done my graduate work on police and I spent a lot of time with narcotics officers on the south and west Sides of Chicago. I saw how beautiful

---

* *For an interesting race-based critique of regionalism, see Gary Delgado, 'Colorlines' (September/October 1999)*

those neighborhoods once were and how devastated they were now. And I saw the same thing starting to happen in Minneapolis. It had been a workingclass area and when I came back it was increasingly poor and segregated.

So I started talking to my brother Gary. He had written a book called *The Closing Door* and that had a huge impact on me. A lot of it was about the inner suburbs of Atlanta. I had been working as a county prosecutor in Minneapolis and we got a lot of cases from inner suburbs up here, places like Brooklyn Center and Columbia Heights. There were a lot of poor people in the suburbs having the same problems in the city.

So I started to measure all these things. I started to measure where the poor suburbs were, and I started to measure where the rich suburbs were. I talked to a guy named John Adams who had been studying the demographic trends up here and he started to show me maps. The maps were so powerful, I went to the state legislature and said "We have to make maps!"

All the map-making computer programs were too expensive, except for one which was $750. I bought it with my own money and I started making maps of the Twin Cities region. I made about 600 maps in all. And they were largely about separating the inner, older suburbs from the wealthy, white-collar suburbs. In the inner suburbs, the average income was $26,000–27,000. In the white collar suburbs, it was $50,000–60,000. In the inner suburbs, the rate of poverty was more than 10% and rising. In the wealthy suburbs, it was less than 5% and falling. The tax base and services in the inner suburbs were stagnant or declining. The tax base and services in the wealthy suburbs were high and rising. So the maps were about breaking that monolith of the suburbs.

People tend to think of Minneapolis as a white city. When I went up there, someone took me to the ghetto. I was like, "Where? Where is it?"

That's partly true, but the schools are 60% minority. And schools are usually a precursor to what's going to happen in a generation to the population as a whole.

You talk about the tacit agreement, or blackmail, that has gone on between the wealthy suburbs and cities where, basically, "We'll keep poor people here if you send us money." And at the same time in Minnesota cities and older suburbs are sending money to the rich exclusive suburbs who get 85% of the highway money and tons of free sewer money. Who's paying more in this insane bargain?

If you look at raw dollars, it's close. It was a bargain struck in the '60s and '70s, and now there's no way to maintain payments into the city because the suburbs won't pay for it. When you concentrate poverty, essentially you're paying to polarize the society and make these problems more intractable. The moment you talk about the city solving these problems alone, it's like cutting the arms and legs off. Cities need allies.

We need to let the declining suburbs take the lead, because the cities are a curse politically. You can't get anywhere talking about "Save the City." Politics is increasingly about welfare and crime and the failure of social programs and things associated with cities. The wealthy suburbs are firmly Republican. The battle for the middle is these poor, older suburbs. These people are really hurt and they're really angry. These are the people who are being downsized. They're considered expendable in the world economy. They're losing their pensions. They're losing their benefits. They're really angry and they're the swing vote. They elected Nixon, and they elected Clinton.

You talk about three very different kinds of suburbs.

The other allies are low tax base suburbs at the edge of the region. They probably view themselves as becoming better off. They're striving to pay their mortgages. But their tax base is low and they have some of the highest high-school dropout rates in the region. They're strapped for cash, they have high infrastructure costs and they're never going to be able to attract many more resources.

You're always trying to find common ground with your opposition, even when they're throwing mud at you, calling you names and making all kinds of unfounded claims. What has been the personal toll on you for maintaining your civility in the face of such underhanded tactics?

Not much. I just proceed ahead arguing the facts. If you looked in the newspaper reports, I think you'd find I haven't spoken badly of anyone.

Who's your audience for the book?

Hopefully people who care about these things, inner-suburban governments. Part of the message is that people from the city have to make some friends in the suburbs and start reaching out and building coalitions. Churches have been very interested, environmentalists, good government people, a lot of groups.

Aren't you afraid that if you succeed in creating more regional cooperation and openness, the rich people who don't want to cooperate and join society will just leave the region entirely and build their own gated fiefdoms where only the rich can go?

I don't think so. There are a lot of benefits to living in a region for wealthy people. They need a regional economy to sell their products and regional transportation to get their goods to market. They need an educated work force which is a regional issue. They need poor people to work for them. We're just saying that regionalism is a two way street. You get benefits and you have responsibilities. The Met Council used to not allow communities to be gated. Now there's one gated community because the Met Council has gotten weaker.

What are you working on now?

We've got a bill to have the Met Council elected instead of appointed, which I think will solve a lot of our problems. It's sponsored by the two most conservative members of the House. In 1994, we made the Met Council much stronger—the conservatives think the Met Council is horrible. They think it's taxing too much so they at least want it to be elected. And they're afraid if we get a Democratic governor in '98, that I might be appointed to head the Met Council. And they certainly don't want that. *[Since this interview, Reform Party member Jesse Ventura was elected governor; no appointment has resulted for Orfield.]*

All the liberals in the audience—we told them not to say anything. All we talked about was how much the Met Council was taxing and that it needed to be elected. It's a tenuous coalition so we're not pushing any other bills this session. As soon as you mention lowering barriers to affordable housing or tax-base sharing, all the divisions come to the surface.

What can ordinary people who aren't state legislators do about the fiscal disparities, political fragmentation, affordable housing barriers and stupid land-use planning in their regions?

Metropolitan movements are beginning all over the country. We have to stop talking about cities and suburbs. I never let people talk about cities and suburbs around me anymore. I always say, "Which suburbs are you talking about?" Half of my friends live in the suburbs. A lot of the progressive forces in the city are fighting with each other over a declining pie. Metropolitan reforms are not an alternative to existing city programs—they are compliments that would gradually reduce overwhelming central-city problems to manageable size and provide resources for community development through metropolitan equity. (1997)

An Interview with James Howard Kunstler
A WICKED CIVILIZATION

When I met the mayor of Milwaukee and he bought Bomb the Suburbs, he also gave me a book called The Geography of Nowhere by James Howard Kunstler. It is the real Bomb the Suburbs, a critique of suburban planning.

Where Rusk and Orfield are politician-scholars, Kunstler is a prophet of doom.

Rusk and Orfield look at cities and suburbs on a political and statistical level: Poverty, crime, inequality, tax-base, low-income housing.

Kunstler looks at beauty, design, civic and community life, spiritual nourishment and the long-term economic and ecological costs.

Rusk and Orfield want regions to share in the suburban dream with more city-suburb cooperation, regional planning and resource sharing.

Kunstler sees suburbanization itself as a major threat to America. "The living arrangement Americans now think of as *normal* is bankrupting us economically, socially, ecologically, and spiritually. The physical setting itself—the car-toon landscape of car-clogged highways, strip malls, tract houses, franchise fry pits, parking lots, junked cities and ravaged countryside—is not merely a symp-tom of our troubled culture but in many ways a primary cause of our troubles."

In his first book, *The Geography of Nowhere*, Kunstler popularized New Urbanism, a movement of urban planners who seek to replace suburban sprawl, single-use zoning and mandatory car use with traditional neighbor-hood design that looks more like a small town. "Main Street U.S.A. is America's obsolete model for development—we stopped assembling towns this way after 1945," writes Kunstler. "The pattern of Main Street is pretty simple: Mixed-use, mixed-income, apartments and offices over the stores, moderate density, scaled to pedestrians, vehicles permitted but not allowed to dominate, buildings detailed with care and built to last....It produced places that people loved deeply."

The sequel, *Home From Nowhere*, combines more tongue-lashing of sub-urbanization with his eclectic (mainly conservative) social views, personal sto-ries, and a running account of New Urbanisms' battles and small successes at creating traditional neighborhoods in an age of suburban sprawl.

I love his books because they show me in technical terms what I already feel in my heart: Neighborhoods and small towns feel alive and lovely while strip malls, high-rises and sub-divisions feel dead and disheartening.

How did you get from fishing, painting, riding motorcycles and working for Rolling Stone *into the technicalities of urban planning? How did you even start to become aware of what was going on?*

Kunstler: I'm like a trout who starts to notice there's water around him. Trout don't know they're in water. They don't know it's wet. It's a little hard to date my awareness of this stuff. I guess it started when I was a teenager. My parents were divorced. My mom lived in Manhattan and my dad lived on Long Island. This was in the '60s and you could see the juggernaut of suburban sprawl gobble up Long Island—this beautiful corner of the U.S. During my childhood it completely disappeared. Then, when I went to college upstate, I saw the juggernaut was starting to reach into the provinces with strip malls and subdivisions. After that, I was a newspaper reporter in Albany and the newspaper office was located in this enormous mall that was killing downtown Albany and Schenectady and the activity in those cities. That was in 1973, the year of the Arab oil embargo. I was dependent on my car as a reporter and it made quite an impression on me.

I began to realize a whole body of knowledge called civic design was mak-ing a reconnection with a whole body of historical knowledge that had been thrown away in the Twentieth Century...about the way to assemble a human habitat that is politically equitable, socially and spiritually satisfying and equal to our aspirations as humans. It was a very important break with some 20th century operating principles. They rejected a culture of quantification for a culture of quality and character.

Who were the main people?

The most influential were Andres Duany and Elizabeth Platter-Zyberk. The circle began to coagulate into an organization, the Congress For The New Urbanism. They began to develop a comprehensive, coherent, point of view about what was going on in the country and what needed to be done about it. This group of people enabled me to find a gateway into understanding a bunch of rather complicated issues. Issues that are still baffling and bewildering to most ordinary Americans.

Like what?

A great deal of the stuff in our everyday world is the way it is because it has been designed by bean counters . . . traffic engineers, people who are very narrow, empirically driven. A traffic engineer operates from the standpoint of making cars happy—so you get streets that are designed to make cars happy. The New Urbanists decided that wasn't good enough. We needed a better set of standards. One thing they asserted was that it was better to put the place we call home near the place we call work and the place we call shopping and the place we call entertainment like in a small town—and that the whole regime of mandatory commuting was insane.

What has been the response among urban planners?

Predictably, a certain number have gotten excited about the prospect of doing things better. A certain number are the classic old guard that refuses to let go of a dying worldview. And there are people in the middle who are susceptible to having their minds changed. Even the traffic engineers and developers have to live in the same shitty environment as everyone else. Many had no idea there was something better, but many of them realize the current way is a costly and toxic program. There are very few people in the United States who don't realize auto use is out of hand to some extent. Even the people who love suburbia complain about traffic. They just think we need to build more highways and parking lots.

We've had only one way of evaluating the cost of cars to society and that is to quantify air pollution. We count up the number of carbon particles per cubic foot and that becomes our sole measure of the harm caused by cars. Unfortunately, there are many repercussions that are extremely difficult to quantify. How do you quantify the social damage to a child who has to be chauffeured around for her entire childhood, who never learns to navigate her everyday world by herself? A 14-year-old girl who has never had to get home from the library by herself. The damage to millions of children over the last forty years, in essence, to their personal sovereignty.

How are you saying this damage is manifest later in life?

One of the clearest ways is the decay of the idea of the Common Good in favor of extreme individualism. The idea that the only thing that matters is your personal interest. You don't have responsibility to the public interest. We live in a childish way with no regard for future generations, which means we disrespect the present—not to mention the past. This shows up in some interesting ways. One is manifest in local political debates. People who call themselves conservatives are opposed to building small towns in the American tradition. I was giving a slide show in a small town in northern Michigan. This seventy-year-old county commissioner stood up and said people had the God-given right to live on two acres as the zoning specified in the town. I said that there was another, older model in their own town and that their best residential street in town was actually an example of it. This asshole said to me, "Some people don't want to live in a goshdarn commune." I said, "If you think the best street in your town is a commune, you're a disgrace to conservative ideology. You don't even recognize your own best traditions." I told him he was a dangerous radical.

What about other reactions?

Now that I've been on the circuit for awhile, the old guard is starting to attack me. Alex Garvin, an old academic fossil from Yale, gave me a bad review in the *New York Times*. He said something like [whiny voice], "Mr. Kunstler thinks we have a problem with cars in America. A lot of Americans would disagree with that." That's like saying, "Mr. Kunstler thinks we have a problem with heroin in America. A lot of heroin addicts would disagree with that."

I tell people we have become a civilization of clowns. Some people are offended by that, but just as many people recognize that it might be true. As a civilization, we're no more special in the eyes of God than the Romans or the Spanish in the Fifteenth century or the British in the Eighteenth century or the Aztecs or any other once-great civilization. This idea that Americans in the Twentieth century are the apex of human development is very childish. We're a childish and wicked people who deserve to be punished.

And how do you picture that happening?

By losing some of the goodies we believe we are entitled to. Like the right to eat a fatty diet with no consequences, the idea that we have no responsibility to our fellow man. That represents behavior we will pay a price for. We will pay a price for our excessive love of cars with global warming. We're already paying a price for suburbia in loss of community and civic life. Unfortunately there hasn't yet been an economic or political crisis that has forced us to re-examine the way of life we've chosen, but I believe there will be one within the next 25 years.

What's your basis for saying this?

Economist Lester Thurow's new book says a lot of the same things. The growing disparity between the rich and the poor is going to severely challenge our democratic institutions, because people will lose faith in them and their ability to mitigate the economic distortions of a free-for-all market economy. We've already entered a period of cultural meltdown. I think that's reflected in the sadism and brutality of our pop culture. But I do foresee the possibility of a cultural transformation. Sooner or later, we're going to enter a more culturally rigorous phase of history in which our standards and expectations will be raised in everything from art to personal behavior. There are cycles of order and disorder in human events and sooner or later our age of disorder will come to an end and a new consensus will form out of the accelerating chaos of the present day.

And you see us becoming more compact and pedestrian-oriented like European towns and cities?

Urbanisticly speaking, Europe is way ahead of us. They use up about half as much energy per person. European towns and cities offer a quality of life so superior to that found in the U.S. in some respects that it's like the difference between the way hogs live in a pigsty and the way humans live in a house.

(1997)

How Our Fear of Crime is Killing Us
BETWEEN PRISON AND THE GATED COMMUNITY

His dog started barking furiously. It was the middle of the night. He lived in Northbrook, a wealthy suburb outside Chicago. There was an intruder trying to get in the front door! He got his gun and started shooting. He shot the intruder to death. When he turned on the light, he discovered that the intruder he shot was not an intruder at all but his daughter Lesley returning home from college unexpectedly late on a Friday night.

This is not some urban legend but an actual tragedy that happened to my mother's cousin several years ago. It is a graphic illustration of a complex phenomenon in America today: our fear of crime is killing us. Our fear of crime is a fear of young black and Hispanic men, of strangers, of streets, of cities, of ghettos. It sucks us down into a spiral of fear—the engine behind the decline of our civic and community life. The end of Lesley Horberg's life.

The spiral goes like this: White and middle-class fear, white and middle-class flight, flight of jobs and capital, shrinking tax base, degradation of public services, accelerated suburban sprawl, destruction of countryside, race and wealth polarization, regional polarization, higher cost of government, declining public institutions; less contact between rich and poor, top-down poverty

programs rigged to fail, more hostility toward the poor; more industries that exploit fear, prison guard and construction unions that benefit from fear, more laws that exploit fear, more fear in the media; less opportunities for poor people, more desperation, more crime, more public fear, tighter security, less community life, less public life, less political participation, worse politicians, and less support for the common good.

The cancer of fear has taken over. We have government by fear. We have a fear economy. We have a landscape of fear. We have a mass media that sells it. Any effort to reverse the spiral of fear must begin with individuals taking initiative to examine their own fears, asking whether their emotions are being manipulated, and taking bold steps to test the validity of their fears. Then a grassroots movement can be built to transform the culture, government and economy.

The black community has been arguing for decades whether middle- and upper-class blacks should move out of the ghetto to more suburban and white neighborhoods. But I want to raise a question that I've never seen raised by anyone on the political spectrum, either black or white, rich or poor, Why isn't it good for middle- and upper-class whites to live in the ghetto?

Millions of ordinary, middle-class Americans still live in ghettos. Thousands of middle-class *whites* live in ghettos. I personally know at least 20 of them. No, they are not clowns. They don't even consider themselves brave. At least half are female. Occasionally they get beaten up or robbed, but not any more than middle-class whites who don't live in the ghetto. Not one of them has been shot, stabbed or raped because they lived in the ghetto (although a few of them were raped in non-ghetto areas).

This is not because ghettos are good places. They are bad places which are created because race and class-based disinvestment and discrimination by white and middle-class people, who move away from neighborhoods and pull up the ladders of access to the networks of opportunity and economic self-advancement that middle- and upper-class people take for granted.

But there are good things about ghettos. They preserve the sense of neighborhood and community that were once typical of urban life—knowing your neighbors and shop owners, a sense of history and extended family, the fabric of casual encounters, street, stoop, and public transit life, charm and compactness of buildings, the opportunity for small business, and the pedestrian as opposed to automobile scale. All the things that used to make city neighborhoods feel like small towns—even as our urban planners, government and business elites have replaced them with high-rises, strip malls and parking lots.

Ghettos serve as a shield against the arrogance of the affluent world. Yes, there is still the landlord, the teacher, the cop, the pawn shop owner, the social worker—all the missionaries and pimps of poverty—but there's still a sense of belonging, a sense of familiarity and place and community, a cultural comfort zone. That's why gangs fight to protect neighborhoods they don't even own. That's one reason so many kids of color who go to white schools feel torn apart inside. That's why gentrification is a bad word.

Affluent people, especially affluent whites, don't know how to live in the city. They don't get to know their neighbors. They don't talk to strangers on the street. They drive everywhere. They don't shop in local stores. They don't get involved in grassroots community groups, or if they do, they try to take them over. They're uptight, defensive, patronizing and self-congratulatory about every little thing they do. They don't bother to really get to know people and let people really get to know them. They don't learn the hard and deep lessons people have to teach them. They don't become part of the village. They put up a fence instead of sitting on the stoop. They call the police on neighborhood kids. They get offended and scared. They *attract* panhandlers. They don't share. And they bring in more affluent people who drive up the rents and price the residents out.

In Chicago, the "inner-city" isn't the location of the ghetto anymore. Almost everything within 20 or 30 blocks of downtown has been gentrified or is about to be. The new location of the ghetto is the outer-city and the inner-suburbs. Many other cities are trying to follow a similar pattern. If they do, it will only succeed in moving our ghettos into the suburbs (the way they are in most third world countries), and destroying the soul of the city.

Any progress toward more livable communities must begin with our fear of crime. The good news is, if you're white and middle-class, most of your fears are not supported by facts. As Minnesota State Representative Myron Orfield wrote, "Minnesota planning found in 1994 that residents of Hennepin and Ramsey Counties held expectations of victimization that were in some cases more than six times their true likelihood of victimization." In most instances, when we jump out of the Fear Box, we will be pleasantly surprised to find that crime isn't nearly as bad as we imagine. Americans are afraid of crime because we aren't cultivating community life and cross-cultural social skills, we watch too many scary TV shows, and we have no sense of statistics.

Here are a few statistics that begin to tell the story.

For all our fear of crime, the FBI reports that almost half of all Americans have never even been *punched*. Chicago, where I live, has less than 2.5 murders per day for a population of 2.7 million people. Most of that remains within the violent subculture of a relatively small group of people. Even if you live in the ghetto, as long as you stay out of the bullshit, the chance of being randomly murdered on any given day is less than one in a million. Most Americans take a greater risk everyday just by driving their cars.

When I think about how out of hand our fears have become, I wish I could go back in time fifty years before we became a suburban nation when the fear economy was still in its infancy. Back then, cities were in a better position to defend themselves. I try to look into the future and think which of the disasters of tomorrow are in their infancy today. The new growth industries are gated communities and prisons. These are the models for urban life in the 21st century. We will become a nation behind bars. For the time being, people not behind bars are still a majority in this country, but we're losing ground fast. If we don't build a movement soon to save and revitalize our public life, then the cities and the suburbs of today are going to be history.

For those of you who already live in gated communities, I hope there's some way to convince you to join society—while there's still one left to join. It seems our nation is spiraling gradually into fear and darkness. And when the light comes back on, we may be startled to learn the identities of the victims.

HIP-HOP LEADERSHIP

WHO'S REALLY SAVING OUR CITIES?*

If it was a youth service agency, it would be doing a pretty good job.

It gets young people food, jobs, bus fare. It finds them mentors, helps them become entrepreneurs. It gets them off drugs, out of hating themselves, out of abusing their kids, out of gang-banging . Other youth service agencies refer clients to it. And it receives praise. This year alone, it has been featured glowingly in half a dozen publications including *Newsweek,* and the major motion picture, *Love Jones,* was based on the people who hang out there.

What would you guess is the annual budget for an organization that accomplishes all of this?

No. They have no money, no brochures, no pictures of "clients" smiling on the wall. They have never even gotten a grant—then again how would they get a grant? Their phone keeps getting disconnected and they don't even own a computer. They do have e-mail but they have to pay the local copy store to use it. That's because *it*—Literary Explosion ("Lit-Ex" for short)—is not a youth service agency.

Technically, Lit-Ex is a for-profit bookstore, but only in name—it never turns much of a profit. Operating out of a tiny basement for the last five years, it is an epicenter of intellectual, artistic, social, economic and political life in Chicago, a marketplace for homemade goods, and the location of Another Level at Lit-Ex, a weekly series of hip-hop and erotic poetry.

Every one of the volunteer staff who owns and runs Lit-Ex—a core of four to ten men and women under 30—lives below the poverty line but they never have problems with shoplifting. Most have been homeless, but no one thinks of them as homeless because they always have a place to stay. "When I look back, I don't even know how we fucking made it," says founder Kendall Lloyd. "If someone asked me to write a business plan to franchise this, I would have to say 'no' because I don't even know how we did it. Sometimes it's still a mystery where the rent comes from! We wish we could do more for the community—like getting people medical and dental care, but we don't even have medical insurance ourselves. Matter of fact, I need some teeth work right now."

Lit-Ex has never been written about as a youth service organization before because no one thinks of it as a youth service organization, not the people who run it nor the youth they serve. This is the hip-hop you never hear about—the

---

This was originally published in Who Cares magazine in 1997. Many people quoted here have changed their jobs since then.

vast majority of young, low-income artists—who don't have a record deal and haven't shot anyone.

Most haven't finished college or even high-school and very few have any formal organizer training. Still, they throw alcohol-free parties and poetry readings, build recording studios, launch micro-enterprises, paint community murals, hold break-dancing sessions, persuade each other to abstain from sex or wear condoms, break up fights, get each other jobs, learn computers, stay out of trouble or get each other into more benign forms of trouble than they might otherwise be into, and publish magazines. Most have never been interviewed in any capacity—let alone as community leaders.

Hundreds—perhaps thousands—of micro-organizations like Lit-Ex spring up in America's urban landscape every year. What's rare about Lit-Ex is that it has lasted so long. Most young, low-income people who try to save their communities for free get discouraged, burnt out and overwhelmed by personal pressures. But this raises the question, if organizations like Lit-Ex can do so much with so little, why aren't they getting support from foundations and more established nonprofits? And how can they attract resources to do more—and to survive—without compromising or polluting their intimate connection with their base?

HIP-HOP AS A DOUBLE-EDGED SWORD

From the beginning, hip-hop's unstated goals were not that different from the stated goals of many community-based youth organizations. Hip-hop grew out of the South Bronx gang culture of the early '70s—the astounding evolution in less than a decade of DJing, break-dancing, rap and graffiti—as a reaction and an antidote to the drugs, violence and cynicism of the post-Black Power era.

Graffiti caught on in Philadelphia in 1968 and in Harlem in 1970. DJs began throwing outdoor "park jams"" in the South Bronx a few years later. Rap evolved from MCs—the hosts—of the park jams. Break-dancing came from the dancers who would dance on the "breaks" of the songs. Afrika Bambaataa, himself a DJ and a leader of a gang called the Savage Skulls, brought the four elements together as "hip-hop" under a new organization, The Universal Zulu Nation, whose motto was "Peace, Unity, Love and Having Fun." The Zulu Nation was supported by a community center in the Bronx River Projects until the mayor decided to shut them down.

Hip-hop gained a worldwide following in the '80s and rap reached maturity with lyricists like Rakim, MC Lyte, KRS-ONE, De La Soul, Latifah and Public Enemy who made it cool to be righteous, use big words, study history, and become politically and spiritually attuned. Throughout the '80s, to varying degrees in different locales, hip-hop served as a bridge from crime, drugs and madness to work, creativity and citizenship. Hip-hop got kids out of their neighborhoods, introduced them to different cultures, provided an arena to learn at their own pace, set their own goals and succeed on their own terms. In many circles, it is almost cliché to say, "Hip-hop saved my life."

In its informal, impossible-to-document way, hip-hop culture probably did as much to keep young urban males off of drugs, out of fights, and constructively engaged during the 1980s as all the at-risk youth programs combined.

But hip-hop has always been a double-edged sword, reflecting the best and especially lately, the worst of urban America, with the murders of Tupac Shakur and Biggie Smalls. "When rappers first proclaimed themselves great, that was a huge dissenting opinion in a society which said they were irrelevant, the scum of the Earth," explains Jay George, an Oakland-based rapper who co-directs Rising Youth for Social Equity (RYSE), a youth empowerment agency. "But we have failed to become a complete, viable counterculture. When it comes to our treatment of women, we're still on the same page as the U.S. culture. It mirrors the ruling class. Rappers want to drive around in a Lexus dressed like a banker."

Rappers feel most of the negative attention they receive is unfounded. "When I mention hip-hop to older people, there's a visible knee-jerk reaction in their face," says Rha Goddess, a lyricist who grew up on hip-hop and returned to it after a successful run in corporate America and a string of nonprofits. "What intimidates people is the boldness, the honesty of it. There are some very nasty and ugly truths about this society and people are not trying to hear it. Sure there's some hip-hop that glamorizes the gangster lifestyle, but there's a lot of hip-hop that if we read between the lines, we should learn that there's a lot of rage among people who are poor and marginalized. Hip-hop is the wake-up call."

As the hip-hop generation matures, many recording artists and industry executives—like their grassroots counterparts—are beginning to realize they have responsibilities to their fan base.

"When Dr. King led the Montgomery bus boycott, he was 26 years old, younger than Puffy and RZA," says Bill Stephney, C.E.O. of StepSun Records. Stephney is also engineer of the Ready to Live Foundation—a reference to Biggie Smalls' first album *Ready to Die*—which is raising money to fund hip-hop-based grassroots organizations. "Puffy and RZA are putting together economic concerns that are being studied as revolutionary at the highest levels of business schools such as Wharton and Harvard. People are starting to realize that it's not about 'How can we save the kids in the projects?' but how can they save us. We have some of the finest minds for entrepreneurship—the Bill Gateses and Oprah Winfreys—living in those buildings, if they only had the resources. We're always talking about 'protecting the poor'—well that's *dismissive*. If they can create a $5 billion industry from nothing, what else can they create?"

INNOVATIVE STRATEGIES FOR URBAN PROBLEMS

"Before you can tell somebody to get off drugs, to be responsible, to vote, you have to build family, love and culture," says Boston-based Najma Nazy'at, a national consultant on youth programs. "That's what hip-hop is all about. That's why young people are attracted to it, and that's what all these youth programs lack—that's part of why they fail." Still in its infancy, a generation of shoestring organizations is developing nontraditional approaches to old problems. Barrios Unidos, a nationwide Latino gang-truce organization with ties to hip-hop, takes young gang members to Native American sweat lodges for coming-of-age ceremonies which simulate the intensity of gang initiations without the violence.

"I wrote artists a letter that started out 'Dear Cultural Leaders' and they were so moved by that!" says Raybblin Vargas, organizer of the festival We Remember Attica that benefits the Community Justice Center. The CJC is a Harlem-based organization that reintegrates ex-convicts and supports halting prison expansion at the expense of funding for social programs, a major concern in the hip-hop community. "One artist came to me 'No one has ever told me I was a cultural leader before.' We showed them videos to educate them about prisons, and then we got them free studio time to record songs."

Four years running, the San Diego chapter of the Zulu Nation has thrown a "B-boy Summit" attracting thousands of young people from around the planet. "Having parties where we can practice being together without violence, that's change in and of itself," says Jay George, one of many who takes a more nuanced approach to urban social meltdown. The Chicago-based Southwest Youth Collaborative sponsors a summer-long University of Hip-Hop where teenagers take free classes from the underground heroes of Chicago's hip-hop scene.

Having experienced the brunt of urban problems first hand, hip-hoppers often have nontraditional analyses of the problems, "Our government intervened to destroy black political activism in the '60s because it was seen as a threat to America," says Bill Stephney. "The head of the FBI during the 1960s, J. Edgar Hoover, said his goal was 'to prevent the rise of a black messiah.' That has had reverberations for thirty years. That's why hip-hop is all that passes for political activism today. You got a generation of entrepreneurs that doesn't know about politics."

Chief among rappers' concern is their lack of control over the rap industry. "For the last seven years, rap has been used primarily against the community by people who do not live in the community," says rapper Chuck D. "Whenever you continuously project negative images of a community, people start to become the images they see on TV. School systems are pretty much throwing up their hands. A lot of individuals in the music industry and the school system want to do good, but they're part of a machine, so we're setting up a structure for them to do good with little effort."

Chuck D's organization, Rappers Educating All Curriculums Through Hip-Hop (REACH), designed to send rappers into schools, comes along at an opportune time—insurance prices for rap tours have become prohibitively expensive. "REACH can replace the art of the tour," Chuck D argues. "I talked to Tupac before he died. He said *of course* he wasn't going to get up in front of a school and talk about thug life. If someone wants to only do gangster rap, we'll set them up to visit prisons—you're a step ahead of them. But 95–98% of these artists, regardless of their lyrics, are not going to talk about thug life once they get up in front of a school. Have the school budgets subsidize these artists to do the right thing. Understand this, the artist *being there is the step* in becoming accountable to the community."

NON-PROFITS MEET HIP-HOP

Washington D.C.-based rapper-organizer Toni Blackman teaches hip-hop demystification workshops to school teachers. "It is a huge paradigm shift for the teachers," she says. "They have to go around the room and do a rap to introduce themselves. Half of them chicken out, and these are progressive teachers! A lot of adults reject youth culture without realizing it. If you reject a kid long enough, he'll reject you."

Community activists, organizers, service groups and nonprofit managers across the country are turning to hip-hop. "What the nonprofit world can learn from hip-hop is to reach young people in their hearts," says Rha Goddess. "Artists bring the constituency that community organizations are looking for. At the same time, a lot of major hip-hop artists are realizing they don't know a lot about community-building and they're beginning to check for community-based organizations."

Even gangster rappers are trying to publicly act more socially responsible. Snoop Doggy Dogg told L.A.'s *Common Ground,* a hip-hop-based paper for

South Central Los Angeles teens, that he wants to become a cross between Malcolm X, Martin Luther King and Marvin Gaye. One person who has been at the center of creating a synthesis between hip-hop and community work is Donna Frisby, development director at Rock the Vote.

"When I was 21, I was a substitute teacher for a bad, bad seventh grade class in Philadelphia," she recalls. "This was a fairly bright group of kids, some were extremely bright. They were just *bad*. They figured they could just keep acting bad and getting rid of subs. I realized you can't teach them until you gain their trust and respect. I started by asking students what kind of things they would like to see on the wall. I had them bring in things from home. So I had all these posters of hip-hop artists on the wall. Then I got a hold of Kool Moe Dee. I needed to bring in some people they see as their leaders. Of course, the school was not very happy with me bringing in this rapper from New York. They wouldn't put up the money. So I hooked up with Vincent Hughes, a state senator who liked hip-hop. He helped me raise money, and got tickets from the Mayor for Kool Moe Dee to go to the Sixers game and meet Charles Barkley. We also got him radio and print interviews in the local media—made it worth his while and helped him sell records. Kool Moe Dee told my students they needed to be serious about school. He told them he was using rap to get money to go to college. They were very impressed with that. One thing I realized, most teachers cannot communicate with kids. If you're trying to reach youth, you have to understand their music. Don't condemn it. You have to realize when you're not reaching your audience and what you have to change. Instead of just sticking it out and continuing to do it your way, look at who *is* reaching your kids and what's *wrong* with your way."

Some nonprofits are succeeding simply by hiring hip-hop leaders to bring their talents, sensibilities, and reputations into the organization. El Puente, a community-run public school in Brooklyn, hired Edgardo Miranda, a hip-hop artist and activist, to incorporate hip-hop into the curriculum (all 33 of El Puente's first 9th grade class graduated this spring and 31 of them went straight to college). The Point, a community center in the South Bronx, works closely with old-school hip-hop legends Crazy Legs and Pee Wee Dance and graffiti writers Bio, BG, and Nicer. Philadelphia-based Youth Outreach Adolescent Community Awareness Program (YOACAP), a community health and violence prevention organization, hired DJ Woody Wood of rap group Three Times Dope to help them reach teenagers. Wood immediately went around to his friends who were rappers and had them record public service announcements which he played on local radio.

WE ARE THE PEOPLE WE'RE SAVING

Most well-intentioned people who "work with kids"" overlook a simple law of high-school social dynamics: The community-service nonprofit crowd is by and large the same set of people who got good grades and did their homework—the "herbs." Many "at-risk youth" are the "popular kids" who cut school and had adventures —many of them are "at-risk" not only because of their loco home lives, but because they like to take risks. What most not-for-profit leaders fail to grasp is that the "at-risk youth" they're trying to "empower" don't find them any more convincing as adults than they did in high school.

Hip-hoppers, by contrast, are often the most versatile people in any ghetto community. They are friends with the folks most of us avoid on a dark street, not just the comparatively safe go-getters who sign up for an Americorps program. "People call them animals, vandals. But really if you knew them, you'd know they're crying out for love and understanding," says Nikkei Duncan, Deputy Director of the Refugee Project, a foundation set up by Lauryn Hill of the Fugees which does international work in addition to education, and juvenile justice. "Drug dealers are some of the brightest people in our community—ghetto geniuses. My cousin Lamont, when he was 15, he had everyone in the neighborhood working for him. He knew chemistry. He was an accountant. He would take taxes out. He would invest in different things like basketball teams, selling water ices, making money legitimately. By the time he was 20, he got out of it. He sent his brother to private school. We need to take that ingenuity and apply it to something constructive."

Many young hip-hop leaders have been caught up in the madness themselves. "I am the first success story of my AIDS prevention work," says Woody Wood of YOACAP. "I *never* used to wear condoms. How I ended up HIV negative and other brothers ended up positive, I don't know." Born into the trenches, their everyday life is a service—and a matter of survival. "I used to hustle, gangbang, thug life, yo," says Kwadjo Campbell, 25, organizer of The East, a 110-member community development organization in Charleston, South Carolina—and the favored candidate for a city council seat this fall [author's note: he was elected]. "I've gotta be squeaky clean. I live in the middle of the 'hood. My boys, they hustle. One of them is caught up in a murder robbery case. A lot of my family members are out there on that stuff. It makes me a lot more determined. We're uncompromising because we know what time it is, man, because otherwise it's death for our children. This past Saturday, I was just walking through the 'hood and I saw these brothers doing they thing. They said, 'Kwadjo, you running? You got our vote. Get us some jobs so we can get up off this corner and get the man off our backs.'"

Even well-heeled hip-hop organizers have deep connections to the mayhem. One of the most prominent young men in the record industry, Bill Stephney, when he was the head of Def Jam Records, lived in Brooklyn on St. James Place, the same street where Biggie Smalls and Junior Mafia did their hustling. Coming from much the same background, rappers can influence their peers in a way someone outside the culture never could, "We call ourselves The Runaway Slaves because fools out here are still slaves," says Jay George of Oakland. "They want to be massa. You see this on the videos. They want to live in the big house. It's still the same bullshit. We're telling fools it's no longer cool to be complicit in your own oppression."

THE OUT-OF-POCKET SECTOR

Hip-hop is only the most visible part of a larger force mostly underneath the radar screen of the nonprofit world, the out-of-pocket sector. Usually we think of Civic Good stemming from the public, for-profit and not-for-profit sectors. But how do you classify an organization like Lit-Ex that does the work of the nonprofit sector out of their own empty pockets? Call them the fourth sector, the out-of-pocket sector, the invisible sector. Call it poor folks philanthropy—they remain in the trenches 24 hours a day when the paid do-gooders go home.

"When I was 17, we started a teen group called Tent City Teens," says Najma Nazy'at. "Tent City was the name of the development we lived in. We was just chillin'—but chillin' meant you sometimes would do gang mediation, you helped organize block parties, we brought in nurses to talk to us, we baby-sat so mothers could go to work. When management would try to evict a family, we would all get together and write letters. We created a space where teens could help each other grow up. There ain't never been no space for teens to do that."

So much out-of-pocket sector work takes place outside the normal channels—and the normal etiquette of counselor-client relationships typical of nonprofit organizations. Instead, they operate on the street, within families, in friendships. "I'll be on the bus and I'll just start talking to you," says Nikkei Duncan. "I have this light inside of me and it shines on people. When I walk down my block, the crackheads all come up to me, not to ask me for money, but 'Hey Nikkei!' and to talk seriously. I give them the same respect I'd give any other elder, and they tell me how they're getting their life together. I'll walk up to a boy on the corner smoking a cigarette and I'll take it out of his mouth. Nobody checks people anymore. They're too scared. I'm only scared of God. I was on the train the other day and a white man threw down his trash. I was like, 'Pick that up! You know that's wrong.' He was like 'What?' but he picked it up. My mom used to come outside with her bat and clear the corner, stand up to brothers with guns. You have to have guts."

Kwami, 26, of Little Rock, Arkansas has spent $20,000 of the money he made working at a battered women's shelter to finance PHATLIP! YouthTalk Radio, and a variety of side projects including an 800 teen help line, a statewide Young People's Congress and a citizen's police-watch organization. Instead of receiving grants, the hip-hop community has raised and donated millions to established charitable organizations—from Pepper Johnson's celebrity basketball games to Zulu Nation's canned food drives to a growing number of hip-hop artists' foundations, such as Lauryn Hill's Refugee Project. The Stop The Violence Movement alone raised $600,000 for the National Urban League.

Hip-hop-oriented nonprofits are beginning to think they can find better ways to spend the money. After Michael O'Neal was fired from the Urban League and told he didn't fit in, he took a pay cut and started his own organization. "Even though I was fired, I still had all these young people depending on me. I couldn't just leave them, so I started Fathers Inc. the next day." To finance the Boston-based organization which works with young fathers to be responsible for their kids, O'Neal sold both of his cars and chipped in $30,000 of his own money to fund the organization. Recently, the hip-hop magazine *XXL* launched a campaign to try to raise money for him.

DISSED BY THE DO-GOODERS

Young leaders of the out-of-pocket sector say they are ignored by foundations and mistreated by established not-for-profit groups. "Most of these places tokenize and exploit youth much more than they support them," says Najma Nazy'at. "The nonprofit world is very uncreative. The programming is weak— it's garbage. They focus on grants and how they can suck up to an evaluator's ass. Nine times out of ten, they're people who've never jumped in front of a knife or a gun. There's no political accountability in nonprofits. They have youth programs so adults can make money and feel good about themselves while we're out here risking our fucking lives and our families to get the bigwigs paid and niggas like us burnt out."

The youth program that has worked best, says Nazy'at, is Boston's Youth Outreach Program (YOP). "We loved YOP—it was the most amazing thing I've seen in youth work. It was a simple concept: You take teenagers in gangs and have them build community. Adolescents are an untapped population and an ugly population. The majority of kids trained were gang teenagers or high-risk youth. We were already leaders, just not in a positive way. We did peer leadership on the street."

"The program worked *too* well," believes Nazy'at. "All of a sudden, the funding for YOP disappeared and they canceled the program. People don't really want to hear what's wrong. I was put in the newspaper every week as one of the city's poster children. The mayor and the Good Old Boy Network was trying to groom me. They want to pay a group of teens to look good. But once you let them start solving these problems of hopelessness and self-destruction, then a whole group of teens starts believing in themselves and saying what they think. It turned out we was just supposed to smile. Things I say aren't good for me politically because I always get fired when I speak my mind. I've been hungry and homeless before. Losing a job doesn't scare me. They don't want to hear it but I don't really care because I think it's a crime. We've got shitty teen programs because niggas won't open they mouth."

Nazy'at's experience was echoed by almost everyone interviewed for this story. Almost every one of them has been fired or rebuffed by traditional non-profit organizations. Almost none of them has gotten any grants except for small ones that weren't directly related to hip-hop. "The traditional foundations are so disconnected from this culture and these people," says Bill Stephney of the Ready to Live Foundation. "Every other foundation we've talked to, they can't get past 'Why are rappers spouting misogyny?'"

Many expressed caution about not angering potential funders. "So many people are scared and edit themselves while they're talking," says Yvonne Bynoe, publisher of *Full Disclosure,* a magazine to help rap artists understand the music business. "I don't usually discuss hip-hop outside the hip-hop industry because then you end up having to defend every artist. My dealings with nonprofits have been—how can I say this and be halfway diplomatic?—I don't know if they heard what I had to say. From the questions they asked and the questions they didn't ask, I don't know if it was what they wanted to hear. It's usually privileged white people who don't have a grasp of things outside their own insular world. If you don't come in there saying the right buzzwords, then they're not going to deal with you. The black old guard is just as bad. They need to get some new people in there who are gonna be more honest."

HOW TO WORK WITH THE HIP-HOP GENERATION

How to work with a community that feels most nonprofits are working against them? It will be hard to gain their trust, says Donna Frisby of Rock the Vote. "They don't believe in the system. They don't believe it works for them."

Here are some nuggets of wisdom for youth, community, and political organizations in working with the hip-hop generation:

Understand the culture on its own terms. "That's one of my biggest beefs," says Yvonne Bynoe. "People trying to mold us into something without understanding the roots of who we are and without taking the time to learn the culture you're going to 'help.' There are reasons why things are the way they are.

There's a whole group of people in hip-hop who don't think there's any problems within hip-hop. They'll tell you to go and fix your own problems, the things going on on *your* end. We're not the ones flying the planes, bringing drugs and guns into our community. Do your homework. Come out to hip-hop events and parties. Do your fieldwork—that's one of your buzzwords."

Respect their cultural independence. "The community has always supported us because our *mission* is the bottom line," says April Silver of Akila Worksongs, a multifaceted organization working to make hip-hop artists responsible to their communities. "We have to be very careful in dealing with foundations because we have certain things we're not going to compromise."

Trust must be earned on both sides. Most have been burned so many times by people claiming to help them that you may have to steepen your learning curve a lot to even begin to figure out why they don't trust you. And given the history of government interference in community-based organizations, get used to the idea that you, as an outsider, are automatically suspect. At the same time, don't be afraid to ask blunt questions, say what you really feel and call bullshit.

Hire the grassroots leaders to do what they're best at. A lot of grassroots heroes of hip-hop work menial jobs. "These foundations should hire intern grant officers that are down to be in charge of funding grassroots organizations," says Jay George. "I don't know a systematic way of choosing those people—it's hard. You'd probably have to ask around a lot and use word of mouth to see who different crews respect. I say intern instead of grant officer because grant officers have to present funding proposals to the board who probably won't understand what they're talking about, and if a young person isn't ready for that you could be setting them up to fail. I would want it to be a rotating position, like every two years, so the person is coming right in out of the fray."

Help them get technical assistance and navigate bureaucracy. They may not know they need help, or they may be too proud to ask, but even the most sophisticated and well-educated, like Donna Frisby, have had trouble getting support. "When I started Children First, we had a tax ID number but I didn't know enough to know it wasn't a real nonprofit," she says. "Three years later, I learned we didn't have 501(c)(3) status and I had to hire an attorney to plead our case to the IRS and pay three years of back taxes—that really took away from our program."

They need money, but not necessarily a lot. "Too much money's not any better than too little money," says Jay George. "At this stage, no one organization should get more than $100,000 for three years. We need to stay grassroots or else we'll start buying potato chips and stuff just to have a meeting. But on the other hand, I think the money would have to be distributed as democratically as possible to a bunch of groups, not just two or three that are the most established. One of the conditions would be to have a micro-enterprise component so that we can become self-sustaining, not dependent."

Freely share your resources. Party space and office amenities are always in great demand. But don't act like you're doing someone a favor by sharing resources that they should have access to anyway. If you're dealing with someone who already has their ass on the line, but you won't sacrifice too, why should they even begin to trust you to build a genuine partnership?

Be as committed as they are to the long haul. "A million people have come up to me and told me they were going to help me," says Michael O'Neal of Fathers Inc. "Once they realized it wasn't as easy as they thought, they were gone in five minutes."

Most of the out-of-pocket hip-hop organizers interviewed for this article commented on the recent nationwide upswing in hip-hop community work. And none too soon—demographers predict the bulge in births, coupled with the unprecedented proportion of low-income families will create a calamitous social meltdown by 2005, and land a staggering proportion of Americans behind bars, both of prisons and gated communities.

Without a lot of support from established nonprofits, the current generation of out-of-pocket grassroots organizations will become discouraged, burnt-out and cynical about doing good. "Everyone is recognizing things are at a crisis level," says Bill Stephney. "Right now is probably the best time in a very tragic way. We're willing to talk to anyone—Republicans, communists, capitalists, Christians, Muslims, Jews, God—*anyone*. It's all coming out of desperation."

In the late '80s, the movement toward a more positive form of hip-hop spawned the Stop The Violence Movement and myriad other organizations like South Central Love, started by Ice-T. "The problem with South Central Love is that we were unaware that nobody gives a damn," writes Ice-T in the introduction to *Uprising* by Yusef Jah and Sister Shah'Keyah. "Only in a dream world when you're trying to help the community would you think that there's going to be aid from somewhere. That's not going to happen. The bottom line is nobody cares. I went on *Arsenio Hall* and begged for some support; four people called us out of 50 million who saw that show. I had to sit back and figure it out, why wouldn't people call? The first thing I came to realize is that the people who do care are broke. In order to care about a gang member you have to have somebody in your family that's involved in it."

For people who ain't broke, the bottom line is, are you willing to join the family?

an interview with Rha Goddess

MASTER OF COMBINATIONS

Rha Goddess is a master of combinations. She has worked in corporate America (for a chemical company, no less) and she was the highest ranking woman in the Zulu Nation, where she started the Malikas, a rites-of-passage program for young women and girls. She helped found Sista 2 Sista, a Brooklyn-based freedom school and mentorship program for young women of color. She does diversity trainings for corporations and conflict resolution with young people. And she is incredible on the mic. She was featured as a poet on the Eargasms compilation. Her independently-released debut album Soulah Vibe is out. It's hot, and her live shows are like nothing you've ever seen.

Sister, how many different people are you?

Rha Goddess: I think I've gone from being three different people to two different people to one. I'm in an integration phase. I think there are advantages and disadvantages to integrating the different sides of yourself. There was the business woman, the shark, who can be at the table and negotiate to make things happen. Then there's the activist-organizer who serves the communities I am a part of, and then there's the artist who wants to sing about it all and tell stories, but the artist persona is where I'm more spiritual and a lot crazier—and at the same time marry it with the street griot of what hip-hop is. Probably that's my harder edge. I have a hard edge and then a softness musically.

Who are your communities?

I'm part of this community of hip-hop intellectuals. There's street knowledge and then there's academe, the ones who marry both formal and informal education, that are able to process what goes on and some step up and influence it.

Many poets represent that marriage for me. Jessica Care Moore is building an institution with Moore Black Press that's going to be here after she's gone. She's investing in the community and publishing books by other writers, her peers. What she's doing is huge. Part of the reason I'm self-financing my own project is the same reason: We've gotta create more institutions, more community landmarks in our generation. We've gotta leave more for those coming behind us. Otherwise, why are we here? You know what I'm saying? Really. Why are we here, if not to take shit to the next level?

There's probably about 20 of us spoken-word artists who are out of New York but whose audience is all over the country. We understand we need to own our own creativity more than our predecessors have in the past. Not only do we know how to kick that poem, but we know how to do business, and we're focused on our community. There's Medusa in L.A.; Michael Franti in the Bay Area; Malik Yusef in Chicago; Toni Blackman in D.C.; Brothers like Ras Baraka; Yvonne Bynoe, April Silver; the folks who are working on the *No More Prisons* CD; in Boston, Soulflower who's a poet. And then on the straight up street side is my Zulu brothers and sisters. It's all my young people. The people I've had the pleasure of doing trainings with. From Sista 2 Sista in Brooklyn to my young people in Alaska.

And what are you really trying to do?

I asked myself that yesterday, "What are you trying to do?" Heal and empower myself and create opportunities for others to do the same. Empowerment. I know it's a dirty word. But that's what I'm trying to do. I'm trying to bring about transformation and healing.

The role of the artist in a movement is to support the people working on the front lines. There are many artists who support the movement. They are not the leaders of the movement. Not that they don't do things for the community—benefits and teaching and writing workshops. But if you really want to know what's going on, talk to the brother working in the neighborhood. He's the one more likely to get that gun out of that kid's hand. It's not in-your-face leadership. It's quiet, powerful leadership, but in the absence of it being in-your-face, you tend to look at what is in your face.

People look at the artists as the leaders . . .

Right, because we have a whole generation of leadership that has not yet stepped forward. And most of those who have stepped forward are leaves off a dated vine. A lot of this I don't want to get too specific about because I'm not trying to call people out. I don't have a problem with you flossin'. But get down and do the work too. Most true grassroots leaders ain't thinking about being on TV. They're thinking about that kid that didn't show up for a workshop, and they're concerned if they should go look for them. If you want a clue as to how I feel about that, check the lyrics on "Gangsta Religion" on my EP. This thing about the charismatic leader is pretty old. I think the new model is collaborative, dynamic leadership, where everyone is involved, where we develop everyone's strengths. Where everyone can play.

Who do you have in mind who's modeling that?

I give Ras Baraka a lot of props. Ras is one of the few conscious people from our generation who's willing to play in politics and that alone gets you props. He ran for Mayor of Newark, and City Council, and he's a great poet. The level of out-and-out drama and harassment he experienced from the powers that be…it's all about the money. He was brave to go into that arena. They were very threatened by him. The political machine is very threatened by the mobilization of the hip-hop nation. God forbid they become politically savvy. God forbid they know what's going on. Any effort to mobilize this generation, particularly poor people, young people, people of color—even poor white kids because there's some class stuff going on too—it has been blocked, or it hasn't been supported.

Another person who's doing it is Toni Blackman in D.C. Toni's activism looks a little different. It's very grassroots, very steeped in the arts and in spirituality. If you ask me what's her movement, really it's providing access to the art and culture of hip-hop, rather than the industry. And validating it in a very powerful way, working with the Smithsonian. Yes, graffiti does belong next to a Picasso. Toni provides the space for that.

Ani Di Franco is an entrepreneur. She's doing what I'm trying to do as far as "I own this shit." She's got it hands down. She's not going to record companies. Record companies are like a bank. They're investment bankers. They give you an advance and the only other thing they do is handle your marketing and distribution. That's all they do. They tell you how to spend your money. Then you have to pay them back. And they charge crazy interest rates!

How are you perceived by men?

I have a lot of love from men now! And yet I know I occur as very provocative for some men and maybe some women too. I'm a little too in-your-face. I'm clear to most sisters. We're there. The sisters get me. Some brothers get me. The others, I don't want to say I intimidate them—I think that's a very arrogant statement. I want to understand. That's what I'm after. Not to jump to conclusions that they're not that deep, that they're not emotionally mature. I want to understand where they are and what is so provocative about what I'm saying.

What's your relationship now with hip-hop? I heard this song you did where you used all these old words from the '80s. I was like, how many kids are really going to be feeling this?

I know which song you're talking about. It was a classic piece, paying homage to the culture. That's why the terminology was dated. That's why it's called, "The Elements." I'm saying that's what I am. There's people who believe if the music isn't a certain way, then it isn't hip-hop. I'm saying that's bullshit. No. I *am* hip-hop. *Everything* I do is hip-hop. You can't bind me. In that song I say, "Earth, Fire, Water, Air—the elements I don't just do, but am." Who I am is global. My conversation is global. I don't even have to live in this country. I think this whole conversation, this whole awakening, is happening all over the world. We just haven't been in full contact with each other to acknowledge it.

Oh, now I get it. You're saying the four elements of hip-hop are Earth, fire, water, and air, instead of B-boying, MCing, DJing and Graffiti. You're saying hip-hop is broader than we usually think. Before hip-hop was a culture to liberate the minds of ghetto youth, now the way people have narrowed it, it's keeping people trapped.

Yes, but now it's shifting back. That's why it's so profound that we're in the studio right now with KRS, who not only gets it, but is willing to push consciousness through the music industry. He's human. We're all human. But what he brings is much more a rallying call for empowerment than many of his hip-hop colleagues.

We have to support him, support the Roots, Outkast, Goodie Mob, Black Star. The glass ceiling seems to be gold, talking about consciousness. You can't go platinum talking about consciousness. The Fugees and Public Enemy appear to be the only prominent exceptions to that rule.

You see where Lauryn went. Actually, Wyclef went there first with *The Carnival*, moving hip-hop outside of the box. He still didn't go as far as I would have hoped. But it was a brilliant album. I just don't think heads were ready.

But Lauryn's taking it there. She still didn't go as far as I would have liked in terms of her messages, but she takes it there with the way she lives her life, the integrity of her lifestyle.

So where do you place yourself?

I'm very clear that I'm an activist and my music is an extension of my activism. It's just another way I use my God-given talents to make a difference, but it's in service of a larger vision. And I intend to use everything I can see and hear to do that. I'm not doing this because I want to be a star and I don't say that lightly. Not that I won't become a celebrity, but that's not my rationale.

And what other artist-activist that you see is the most like you?

It's funny, but Danny Hoch is probably my soul mate in this game. He's on some shit and I'm right there with him. Danny is very clearly rooted in some identifiable movements. The work that he's doing around prisons. The work that he's doing around Cuba with Black August, breathing life into and validating the hip-hop community of Cuba and challenging the U.S. embargo. He's somebody I'm clear uses his God-given talents for something. My biggest criticism is that he doesn't do more question and answer when he performs. Because a lot more people in the ranks of the white elite are starting to feel Danny's shows, but they don't get it.

What do you mean? What did you notice about his audience?

I had an experience standing on line for his show at PS 122. It was a very white, elite, "Let's see what's artsy and new" kind of crowd. There was a few people of color. And people were looking at me like, "What are you doing here?" There's a particular look. It doesn't happen everywhere I go. And I found it enraging that this was my culture and they were watching it and displaying no respect for the practitioners. But they'll pay $50 to have you entertain us. It was the same thing when Crazy Legs did his show on Broadway, *Jam On the Groove*. I'm real clear that African-American culture is not respected by the wider society, but we can entertain white people every day of the week.

I think it's good that Danny speaks to white people. In a multicultural context, no one can speak to everyone. We need many voices, and sometimes it needs to be white people who do that. Racism is not our problem—it's an illness. Not that it hasn't impacted us. It clearly has, but it's not our problem, nor can we solve it. I think white people have a lot of healing to do, but maybe they're so scared to do it with us around. Some of it may have to be a closed-door family kind of thing.

There are a lot of white people who just aren't comfortable with black people being empowered. And they can blame the black people, or make any excuse, but it's really about comfort levels and power.

Which is why any black person who gains power has to be a master at making white people feel comfortable.

Otherwise white people's paranoia and racial fear will only let them get so far. I think that's very disappointing. I'm not someone who yells racism all the time. That ain't my steez. We all got baggage as a nation and as individuals. And it disappoints me so I'd actually rather not call it that. It's about their fear, and ultimately in the end they lose. They didn't even know what they had. I think that's probably why I do what I do. After having spent six years in corporate America, and four years before that at Vassar College, on a predominantly white campus, I felt very stifled in my own beingness.

And now you do workshops for corporations.

Yes, doing transformational work in corporations is something I have to do. There's no way you could have my identity and be in the places I've been and not do it. There's different schools of thought about how our identities get formed and how to help people transform themselves when they get stuck in a certain behavior. We walk people through a process that's a non-threatening way to get people to look at themselves. It was funny, the first time I ever did a workshop, I got triggered five minutes into it by this guy who said, "There's no such thing as oppression." I got angry. But the thing about being a group facilitator is that it's not about my reaction. It's really about them. And when you're committed to a group, there's no room for you in the room.

Why do companies invite you in to do this?

They want to transform and heal. Often I get called in after something happened as part of the fix-it strategy. Sometimes I am the fix-it strategy.

And what do they want you to do?

Often times, they're not clear on what they want. I try to get them to articulate what they're trying to achieve. And that's 80% of the battle. They have a lot of different goals. A lot of times, they want to become more in line with what their mission statement says they are. If you say you want a diverse staff but you're 90-some percent white, then you have to look at yourself. Or a lot of times they got told about themselves by an employee that left.

So what are your plans from here?

The Goddess Cipher is expanding. We're bringing on new staff. There's a lot of folks playing on the team: Yvonne Bynoe, my sister Kimberly Greene, April Silver, Kim Davis.

Damn, that's an all-star team.

I know. We're building our infrastructure and capacity to take on more, because we have more business than we can handle. We do organizational development, artist development and we do special-events planning and fundraising. Then we do diversity training and conflict resolution through creative expression.

What if anything is holding you back?

Right now, it's capital. Also, I need a good nuts-and-bolts person because—you've been to my house—I spend 80% of my day answering the phone. I need to get creative in getting an administrative person so that I don't have to be chained to the office. Like someone to set up the files and the database. I have a huge need to set up a database. We got people in every different cipher. The question now is how do we capitalize on it? We have people in politics, entertainment, fashion, activism, film, media and technology. What does that mean? What could be possible with the kind of people we are bringing together? We could be the type of folks that could make something happen.

Also, I'm on the whole conversation about being courageous and what it really takes to stand for what you believe in. A lot of what I've been experiencing of late has forced me to constantly question and ask myself what I'm standing for.

You're being offered devil's bargains?

No, not exactly. I'm being challenged by people around me that to be more successful, I have to do it the same way everyone else is doing it. So then the question becomes 'What do I want to achieve?' And where am I standing in that? It's the integrity conversation. There's a belief by some people that what it's all about for me should be being famous, and having the right people like me and that my energy should be spent catering to them.

The power brokers in the industry?

Yes.

So what are you learning?

Sometimes you have to stand by yourself. It can be a lonely place to stand. It can cost you to stand. It can cost you in people—people no longer being in your life. It can cost you money. It can cost you time. It has definitely cost me. And it's going to keep costing me. But I believe you can experience abundance and still have integrity, and it may not look like what everybody else thinks it's supposed to look like.

Contact: Goddess Cipher 718-735-5394 rhagoddess@aol.com www.soulah.web-jump.com

An Interview with John Payne

THE DETROIT MILLIONAIRE
WHO COULDN'T READ

John Payne is not a rapper. Nor a pro ballplayer. He didn't win the lottery. He didn't graduate college. And he never sold drugs. So how does a workingclass black man from Detroit become a millionaire at age 25 without ever learning how to read?

It's a typical Saturday night. John Payne and his fiancé, Connie are out to dinner and a show. They're standing outside the theater, one of those corny suburban megaplexes with 12 movies and a bunch of goofies running around buying things. John and Connie are standing outside the ticket office, staring at movie titles. "All these movies look stupid," Connie says finally. "Let's just go to dinner, go home and read." They walk out of the theater and across the parking lot to Bennigan's. They sit down at a table, look at the menu and talk for a few minutes. Suddenly John gets up from the table. "I don't want to spend my money here. Let's go home and fix some macaroni and cheese." They walk out of Bennigan's and drive back home to Detroit.

Fuck the wine and dine.

John would rather save his money and spend time with his family.

You have never heard of John Payne. No one has ever written about him before. He doesn't usually tell anyone his business. He is a black man from Detroit who made a million dollars by the time he was 25.

Legally.

He agreed to tell his story here because he wants young people in his situation to know that it can be done. And if they're in John's situation, someone is going to have to read this story to them, because until John was 24 or 25 years old, he wouldn't have been able to read this page.

There are so many talented young people fighting to get into the music business now. John wants you to know that the music industry and sports are not the only legal ways for young black folks with no college degree to make a good living.

"He's just the opposite of me, because I used to spend all my money," says John's mother Faye Payne. "And his dad wasn't a saver either. John is just stingy. He said he was stingy because that was the only way he could have something. He basically taught himself. He wouldn't take his girlfriends out to fancy restaurants. He would say 'I can go to the store and buy bread and hamburger and I'll make you two hamburgers and still have bread left over!'"

John started early in business, selling candy in school. When he was ten, he asked for a set of clippers for Christmas, and started cutting hair. He worked at McDonald's and Burger King, biking across Detroit to save money on the bus. By the time he was 17, he had opened an Individual Retirement Account (IRA) at the bank.

But school was a different story.

"As far as reading, I never took to it," John says. "I faked my way through school without ever learning how to read. I escaped because I was a clown. I'd get myself kicked out of the class, messing with the other kids or talking back to the teacher. I had a memory so when they would go down a list of words for a spelling test, I would memorize them, and at least average a B or C just off memory."

Most of his teachers never figured it out. "I don't think people knew. And if they did know, they didn't do anything about it. A few of 'em knew. Once a teacher would find out, they wouldn't call on me to read out loud. They wouldn't want to embarrass me. Then in high school, reading aloud was never a criteria. I ain't learn shit in high school. I became a basketball player, so I was a jock. I graduated on the honor roll."

"He Couldn't Do Anything Without a Degree"

The only people who knew he couldn't read were his parents. His mom did his homework. She got him tutors, but they never worked out. His mother didn't know what to do at the time. "When I got older, I realized what was really going on." says Faye Payne. "When I was younger, I didn't understand. How angry and frustrated they get because they can't read the words. But now I work with foster children. Most of their disabilities in school is reading. So many black males, that's why they're angry at the world."

John was accepted to college in California on a basketball scholarship, but he still couldn't read. "When I was in college, my girlfriend would say, 'Why don't you never write me?' I used to pick out cards."

His basketball coach found out he couldn't read. "He got me three tutors. In that one year of college, I learned more than I had in my entire elementary and high school. By the time I got to college, I wasn't as ashamed of it no more. I was fed up. They had labeled it dyslexia. My coach said, 'That's bullshit!' If I coulda stayed in college four years, I'da been straight. But they cut the basketball program after my freshman year and I went back home to Detroit."

When he got back, he told his mother that he didn't want to go to school anymore. He wanted to be a barber. "I wanted him to get a college degree to be a teacher, or a degree in business," says his mother. "Because I know he couldn't do anything without a degree. And he said, 'Nope. I tried it for you but this ain't what I want to do.'"

John got his barber's license when he was 20. His first job was at a salon on Nine Mile Road in the heavily Jewish suburb of Oak Park that black people were just starting to move into. He was the first black man to work there. "They had me at a chair in the back cutting all white people's hair. I was fucking it up! So I went and got my flyers out. I took flyers up to the high school. Black people started coming in and sitting at the front of the shop. The more black customers that came in, the more we lost white customers. I cut hair, saved my money. Finally, the owner, this old Jewish guy said, 'You can buy the shop!' Before you know it, after a year I bought the shop for $5000. I had saved up $15,000. It was a three-chair shop. I turned it into a ten-chair shop."

Flipping Haircuts into Real Estate
John had never been into real estate before.

He was about to move out of his father's house and start paying rent.

But his father asked him, "How much are you paying in rent?"

"Five hundred dollars."

"How much rent you pay in a year?"

"Six thousand."

"How much you gonna pay in five years?"

"Thirty thousand."

"You better save up and buy you a house."

So John told his wife at the time that he was interested in real estate. "She hooked me up with this crackhead named Willie Prince, who was her uncle. He showed me a list from Volunteers of America for all these abandoned properties. I bought five houses for $5000. Willie Prince knew how to fix up houses. He knew everything. The first house we went into, the first thing he did was stick his hand in a damn sewer. I thought it was disgusting! Pretty soon, I was doing it.

"The first house we bought, the whole basement was flooded with feces. Willie took two crates, slid across the basement on them, reached down into the sewer, pulled out a sock, and all the shit just drained out. Someone had wiped themselves with a sock! The first family that lived there, I would have to bring them toilet paper every week. People would wipe themselves with newspaper, leaves, anything! And I used to bomb their house for roaches. The woman had five kids. I used to bring them Christmas presents until they got taken away by the state."

The crew of John, Willie, and their other friends Gil and Roosevelt fixed up houses cheaply. He bought all used toilets, used windows, used doors. They fixed up a house a week. They fixed up 12 houses and had tenants living in them within a year. The following year, they did five more houses. And the following year, which was 1995, John had 25 houses. In 1996, he bought another barbershop.

It isn't easy being a landlord in Detroit where people commonly steal aluminum siding off of houses for scrap metal. Although John says he's never been robbed, he goes through a lot of problems with tenants. "I was evicting a girl and she said, 'Motherfucker, I'm gonna show you you don't just evict me.' I said, 'What you mean by that?' She said, 'You'll see.' I came back the next day. She had burnt the house to the ground, but I got my insurance."

John knows how to protect his ass, but he has had his share of setbacks. His marriage with his first wife ended in a divorce that cost him $55,000. The relationship didn't work with the mother of his baby. And Willie Prince got shot in the head shortly after he finished showing John how to fix up houses.

"Ain't None of These My Ideas"

John thinks up business deals the way some people write raps.

John is explaining all the little businesses he's going to start in his new barbershop, The Buzz, on Six Mile and Livernois (where a fade is still $7), "We're gonna have a little beauty supply right here. A nail technician right here. A candy section over here. And a section for cellulars and beepers up front."

In 1997, John started a small van transport company called Progressive Transportation to take workfare workers to jobs in the suburbs. John's dad runs it. "He worked for the *Detroit Free Press* for 15 years, then they went on strike and hired scabs. We have two vans and a car. Mostly, we take people to and from day care or elder care."

"Ain't none of these my ideas," John says. "Everything I've done is somebody else's ideas. I have a thirst for knowledge. I don't even like being around people who don't stimulate me. Working at a barbershop, you meet all these people who have all these ideas but you rarely find people who move on their ideas. Days turn into years. Man, I gotta make investments! I run into all these people working in a barbershop. I met this guy who wants to get into adult foster care. I said, "We can let you use one of my houses." I cut hair from people from all kind of professions. And I be asking 'em stuff. And they be running it down to me what they do. And so I try to pass it on to other people."

But behind John's business savvy is a deep interest in people and what makes them tick. ""He was always really inquisitive," says his mother. "He learned to do everything not from school. He seems to always connect with the right people."

John agrees, "I'll tell you what saved me. Taking a man for a man. Because Willie Prince was a crackhead. I looked at him as a man because I got something to learn from everybody. Like Dave. People say "Why do you have that crazy motherfucker up in here?" Dave did acid. I ain't did acid. I don't hang around with people who smoke weed, period. Unless, I'm some kinda kin to them. My uncle do drugs. I learn from him about the streets. I'm trying to walk as straight as possible. I play basketball every Tuesday and Thursday at the police station downtown. I'm making some friends down there."

The Barbershop Talk Show

To watch John do anything is to understand why and how he became a millionaire without ever learning how to read. The barbershop is John's personal talk show. Everyone he knows stops by. And everyone he meets, he introduces to other people he knows. Then he asks each person what they think of the other ones. Then he brings what each person said back to the other person's face. This might seem like a dangerous game to play in Detroit, but everyone respects John. He gets away with it.

He has two guests on his show at the moment, his fiancée, Connie, a teacher who is going back to library school, and his uncle Bub, a drug addict in his forties whose good looks and charm have somehow gotten him this far. Bub used to stay at their house until he stole some money. Now John keeps him on a short leash.

"Connie said she don"t want to deal with you today, Bub.""

Bub and Connie sit in silence.

John turns to me later.

"Why do you think I ask everybody what they think of everyone?" he asks. "It's because I don't like to gossip," he says. "I like to have everything out on the table."

"You never gossip," Connie chimes in. "As long as I've known you, I haven't seen you sit up and talk about people."

"Because I don't have to down somebody else to make myself feel good," he says with satisfaction.

"Gil," he says to his electrician. "How long crack stay in your system?"

"Three weeks."

"Bub says three days."

"That's why Bub isn't working now," replies Gil.

I ask Bub what he thinks of John.

"John analyze everything. He a psychiatrist," says Bub.

It's John's show.

Puffy comes on the radio. John is fascinated with Puffy and Master P.

"What's up with these rappers? They getting paid?"

John is cutting hair. He starts imitating Puffy on the radio.

What you want to be?

You want to be brawlers? Shot-callers? Ballers?

Then he starts singing the line from Master P,

Tryna make a dollar outta fifteen cents.

He plays it in his tape deck constantly and repeats it over and over again.

"Tryna make a dollar outta fifteen cents."

John is looking for a pick-up truck. "Hey, I know what I wanted to talk to you about," he says to a friend who stops by. "Take a look at this truck down here. They want $1750. I was gonna offer 'em $1500." Over the course of the day, he asks four different people who stop in to The Buzz to go down the street and have a look at a truck which is sitting outside a derelict-looking auto shop.

Another guy walks into the shop wearing dirty overalls.

"Greasy than a mothafucker!" John says under his breath.

Even though he's cutting hair, you can see his brain working. "Hey man, you work on cars?"

"Yeah."

"Got any pickups?"

Within two days, John has investigated five used pickup trucks and made a purchase.

John has a use for everyone who crosses his path. When I tell him I'm coming to Detroit to write this story about him he says, "Good, I'ma put you to work writing this infomercial and making a pamphlet for me teaching people to buy abandoned property."

Single Dad Learns to Read

It's Sunday. Time to pick up the baby from grandma's house. The baby is John Jr. aka "Jake." Connie is driving. John is sitting in the back with Jake, playing and singing kid songs.

"The itsy-bitsy spider went up the water spout. Down came the rain and washed the spider out. Out came the sun and dried up all the rain and the itsy-bitsy spider went up the spout again..." Then he points out the window at a passing tree. "Look Jake, those are bird nests. What do you think of bird nests, Jake?"

"I've had to be more than just the Daddy," he says. "I'm the Daddy and the Mommy. His mother and I have joint custody, but I am the custodial parent. It takes a lot of getting used to, because a lot of times you want to put your kid off on somebody else when you need to take your kid with you. One guy told me, 'If you can't take your kid with you to the place, nine times out of ten, you shouldn't be there yourself.' I take Jake with me to movies, restaurants, everywhere I go. I take him when I do repairs or collect rent. Jake wakes me up every morning. 'Daddy, I want to eat eat eat.' And he sits on the pot next to me. I call my mom once in awhile when I have a question. One of the biggest mistakes people make is to say, 'I struggled. My child won't have to struggle. My child won't want for anything.' Why would you do that to a child? Struggle is what made you what you are. My child ain't gonna get no special treatment. What do you think of that? Often parents hurt their children more trying to protect them. By my mother caring about me, she wanted to help me—by not addressing the problem."

Buoyed by the confidence of business success, John decided once and for all he would learn to read. "I bought Hooked on Phonics when I was 24. I would get up at six in the morning and practice my words. I was around a woman—the mother of my baby—that was buying me books on tape. What I'm doing now, I can see myself as being a lawyer. I'm 27. I want to be the Mayor of Detroit. But I have to have a thirst for reading to do all that school. I still don't have it. It's a crime how many kids never learn to read. I'm quite sure there's a lot of people in your life right now that can't read. Get a girl's phone number and can't read it. I used to know this guy. He would say 'I'm the X man' You're not the X man. His name was John. He just couldn't read his own name."

Hip-Hop Leadership

- Active Element Foundation 532 LaGuardia Pl. PMB #510 New York, NY 10012 (www.activelement.org)
- LISTEN Inc., 1436 U St. NW #201, Washington D.C., 20009. www.lisn.org 202-483-4494 x13
- Third Eye Movement/Jay Imani, 1230 Market St. #409, San Francisco, CA, 9102, 415-951-4844
- Freestyle Union/Toni Blackman, P.O. Box 73277, Washington, D.C., 20056, 202-387-1248
- PHAT LIP! Youth Talk Radio, P.O. Box 3103, Hampton, VA, 23663. 888-PHAT-LIP
- Akila Worksongs/April Silver, 718-756-8501, www.akilaworksongs.com
- Yvonne Bynoe, yvonne_bynoe@hotmail.com
- Rap Coalition, 111 E. 14th St. #334, New York, NY, 10003. 212-714-1100

THE GREATEST ART FORM OF THE 21ST CENTURY

WHY PHILANTHROPY WASN'T MUCH
OF AN ART FORM IN THE 20TH CENTURY

I get a call from Katie Davis, a reporter who wants to do a program about the Chicago hip-hop community for public radio. It's part of a series on communities. We talked for a long time, she was really cool, and then she asked me a funny question.

"One of the guidelines of our grant is that the show has to be based in a specific community. So I was thinking about doing Wicker Park. What do you think of me using Wicker Park as the focal point of Chicago hip-hop?"

Suddenly it was clear to me. This is one of the many things that foundation people, and the older generation of community-minded folk in general fail to understand about youth culture—its mobility. Yes, Wicker Park is a focal point for hip-hop in Chicago. In some ways, it is the clearest focal point—just as the Village or 125th Street in New York City, or South Street in Philadelphia, or Le Mert Park or Venice Beach in Los Angeles, The Mission in San Francisco or Telegraph Avenue in the East Bay, Five Points in Atlanta, Dinkytown in Minneapolis, Westheimer in Houston, Burnside in Portland, Broadway in Seattle, South Beach in Miami, or U Street in Washington D.C. But most of the people who form the community in those places aren't from there.

And that's just one little tiny example of how foundations don't get it. Why adults who are concerned with community have never been able to organize or to recognize youth subcultures as legitimate communities to be organized and supported, Their unit of geography is off. They think in terms of neighborhoods and cities, and that's fine for a lot of young people. A lot of young people are stuck in their neighborhoods and they do need community centers. But a lot of the most dynamic young people are transient. They're not that connected to one geographical community. Take someone who grew up all over the South Side of Chicago whose family moved to the North Side. Daddy used to stay in the suburbs, but then he moved to Texas. Grandmother lives in Mississippi. Best friend is in the navy in San Diego. Uncle is downstate. Mother is thinking of moving to Minneapolis to be near her auntie. And the kid is thinking about staying with their boyfriend who's going to college in D.C.

How do you fund someone to work with a kid like that?

A lot of our brightest and most ambitious and most at-risk young people are like that. They live all over the place. I meet them on the L train. I meet them on the Greyhound bus, 13–23-year-old kids who are raising their little brothers and sisters. Girls who ran away from home and joined the rave scene.

High-school dropouts with graffiti on their bookless bookbags. Who is looking out for these young people and following them when they leave one place and go somewhere else? We need youth organizers who ride the bus and stay in touch and hook kids up with resources all over the country—not just homeless shelters and runaway centers and soup kitchens. But family. Extended family of people they can relate to. People who listen to them and look out for them and ask them the hard questions about their lives.

You can't employ people to do this. If you put an ad in the paper, you're going to get a bunch of fakers with resumés and credentials certifying them to do youth work, who want to go home and drink a beer at the end of the day. The only way to do it is it be on the streets yourself and know who the people are who are already doing this work out of love and for free. This should be the job of foundations, if they weren't so out-of-touch and into experts and numbers which have nothing to do with the day-to-day lives of America's alienated young people.

A HITCHHIKER'S GUIDE TO COMMUNITY ORGANIZING

And for that matter, what foundation is set up to support any of the out-of-pocket sector leaders you have been reading about in this book?

We need a younger generation of cool rich kids to start an entirely new generation of foundations that supports public transit organizers, and hitchhiker, freight-hopper organizers, and Greyhound bus organizers, and hip-hop organizers, gangster rap organizers, Low rider organizers, cholo organizers, rave organizers, jungle organizers, punk organizers, ska organizers, heavy metal organizers, snowboard, ski bum, surfer organizers, basketball and double-Dutch organizers, skater organizers, druggie organizers, Dungeons and Dragons organizers, gang-banger organizers, graffiti organizers, prison organizers, psych ward organizers, fraternity and sorority organizers, poetry reading organizers, Grateful Dead Phish fan organizers, big hair country music organizers, redneck tobacco-chewing organizers, Goth organizers, mobile-home trailer-park organizers, organizers of people who hang around in parking lots of the local McDonald's, Go-Go organizers, gay and lesbian organizers (amazingly this is the only category that there are paid political organizers of), mall rat organizers, Ani Di Franco fan organizers, organizers of every star who draws a young crowd, vegan skinhead organizers, video-gameroom organizers, ghetto house party organizers, suburban rich kid organizers, lonely kids on the Internet organizers, organizers of young people who appear on televised national talk shows crying out for help, organizers of kids who hang around outside of school and smoke and organizers for subcultures I have never even heard of because I'm no longer 15 years old. Organizers who can actually do something about the madness that horrified so many parents who saw the movie *Kids,* and entrenched political Frankenstein monsters like the military-industrial complex.

The point is not to hire clueless outsiders to "organize"—whatever that means—these groups of young people who are already organized into their own social networks and institutions. And it's not about supporting all these subcultures because they're intrinsically good. The point is to find the young people within each of these scenes who have earned the other kids' respect, but who have a little bit more mature outlook and who are the glue of their respective communities and subcultures and scenes. Those who are already doing the work that schools and drug rehab centers and churches and scout clubs and all of our established governmental and civic institutions have failed to do: Understand and support alienated young people where they're at, as whole people, as mentors and friends, not only to become functioning adults, but to use their experiences to change society. And it's so cost-effective! Instead of hiring one adult with a degree for $30,000 a year to work at a youth center and have a desk, you can support half a dozen young people who are already working from the inside for the love of it, and encourage them not to get burnt out.

WHY ISN'T THERE
A LIST OF YOUTH ACTIVISTS?

Here is another clue that foundations don't get it.

I was recently hired by an organization called Rock the Vote, to work on a campaign they are doing called Rock the Nation. The idea behind Rock the Nation is to highlight young activists across the country who are doing unusual work, and to spotlight them in Public Service Announcements (PSAs) on MTV, BET, and other TV and radio geared to youth. My job is to search the country for young activist groups, in nooks and crannies, under rocks and in the public eye. It's a cool job. I get to be a youth activist talent scout. So my first assignment is to find groups in Philadelphia. I call everyone I know from Philly and ask them for anyone I should talk to who might know someone who might know someone who is a youth activist. Then I went to Philly and wandered around, going into stores and offices, picking up flyers, scanning phone books and newspapers. Stopping people on the street and asking them, *Who do you know that's a youth activist?* Within two days in Philly, and a couple weeks on the phone, I had spoken with about 50 people and collected the names of more than 50 groups, some established, some informal, some youth-led, some adult-led, some radical, some mainstream, some groups that didn't even consider themselves activist groups. I collected names and talked to people until everyone I talked to was giving me names I already had.

Fifty groups, not bad.

And then I said, "Wait a minute. Why reinvent the wheel? Someone must have already done this. Between all the nationwide activist organizations, someone must be publishing a list of youth-activist groups."

Ladies and gentlemen, there is no list.

I checked around and checked around. No one has a list. I mean sure there are lists. Every national group has a list of the local groups it works with. The Center for Third World Organizing has a list of the groups it works with around the country. Youth Action has its list. The Arsalyn Foundation has its list. Students for a Free Tibet has its list. Echoing Green has its list of social entrepreneurs. The Center for Campus Organizing has its list. But no one has compiled a list that considers youth activism as a whole.

The closest we have come is an excellent report in 1994 by Helen Denham for the New World Foundation that profiled about 200 national groups and youth leaders. It was a good survey. But it hardly covered any local groups, where most of the action is.

Everyone wants to start their own little organization or project as if they're the only game in town. There are probably fifty foundations and a couple of hundred organizations that say they are trying in some way to stimulate youth activism. Yet no one has gone to the trouble to pound the pavement and make a list to survey what's already out there.

Hello?

Right now I have the most comprehensive list of youth-activist groups in America. And I barely even had to try. It took me eight months working part-time, a $10,000 budget mostly for phone calls and "making the most comprehensive list of youth-activist groups in America" wasn't even my assignment. I was supposed to be nominating 30 groups for Rock The Vote to feature in its PSAs. The list got made *on the side*.

How come no one has done this before? It's not rocket science. All you have to do is talk to a whole bunch of different kinds of people and ask them who they recommend, and keep calling and calling and calling. I didn't even do a very good job. I just scratched the surface. One of these foundations needs to hire a team of people who will really gather a comprehensive survey of youth activism in America. There's a lot more going on out there than anyone realizes.

CERTAIN THINGS YOU CAN'T PROVE

There are certain things you can't prove in life. I believe that most foundations have their heads up their asses. I can't prove it. It's just what I believe. I also can't prove that I love my mother. I believe that I love my mother. I have anecdotal evidence that I love my mother. I also have anecdotal evidence that most foundations have their heads up their asses.

I can offer nothing in the way of proof.

My first piece of anecdotal evidence that foundations have their heads up their asses is that most foundations only give money to people who apply for grants. My second piece of anecdotal evidence is that most of the people who I have met who I believe are doing the most good with the least resources have never applied for a grant.

How can I *prove* they are doing the most good in the world with the least resources? I can't. How can I prove I love my mother? I can't.

Anecdotally, I can tell you that most of the people I know who I believe are doing the most good with the least resources would have a hard time getting any type of grant. Most of them probably never imagine themselves as deserving of a grant for what they do. Some of them don't own a computer. Almost none of them have 501(c)(3) tax-exempt status. Some of them intentionally avoid taking credit or promoting themselves. Some don't believe in asking anyone for money, or have had bad experiences with money in relationships. Some believe that good human relationships are about love, reciprocity, and interdependence and they feel that applying for grants fosters institutional, lopsided, dependent relationships.

Anecdotally, a lot of the people who I believe do the most good in the world have political or religious beliefs which are seen as controversial. They may be communists or anarchists or Gypsies or Rastafarians or Christian Scientists. Those folks aren't getting any grants! Many do not have high-school or college degrees. Many have menial jobs, are unemployed, or incarcerated. Many get depressed or angry or burnt-out. Many have trouble believing in themselves.

They're not going to apply for any grants.

The second reason I think most foundations have their heads up their asses is their fetish with quantification and "results-oriented" evaluation. This encourages grantee organizations to pursue shallow, unbalanced growth. I believe the job of the philanthropist is to live out the true meaning of the word philanthropy—to invest in *love*. You can't measure love. What are you really measuring? How many clients came in the door? How much their grades went up? You wouldn't choose your husband or wife like that. At least I hope you wouldn't. So why would you apply such shallow measurements of "results" to your funding decisions?

I can't prove it but I believe foundations undermine community by treating people as clients or grantees instead of as friends. Most foundations encourage temporary and superficial service in the form of programs, instead of life-long relationships and associations that weave the fabric of healthy communities. Foundations pay experts big money to study and "solve" other people's problems. They need to get out there and pound the pavement and listen to the people who are *already* solving their own problems and helping their neighbors. And appreciate them and *ask* them what support they need to continue their work.

I can't prove it but I believe most foundations generate a wasteful and backwards infrastructure of grant givers and grant writers. It takes so much energy away from the actual work. Foundations need to find people who are already doing good work. Then *ask* them what they need, and *trust* they'll use it wisely.

I can't prove it but I believe most foundations encourage dishonesty by funding groups that know how to make themselves look good and make problems look simple, rather than addressing the complexity of problems and owning up to their shortcomings.

I can't prove it but I believe most existing foundations have their heads way too far up their asses to even imagine any other way of giving away their money. That's why we need a new generation of people and private foundations to come along who want to invent a whole new field, the art of philanthropy.

WHY PHILANTHROPY WILL BE THE GREATEST ART FORM OF THE 21ST CENTURY

You say good luck convincing foundations and rich people to support the out-of-pocket sector? I say bullshit. Supporting the out-of-pocket sector is the next frontier of philanthropy. There are a hell of a lot more rich people in the world now than there were 20 years ago, we're a hell of a lot richer, and a lot of us are creative, worldly folks.

The problem is, no one ever told us that philanthropy is actually an art form. All we've ever heard is that you write a check to the Alma Mater or some pesky organization to get them off your back. Or if you're old, you have a hospital wing named after you. Not much creativity in that.

When we think of charity or foundations, or nonprofits, or giving back to the community, we immediately think of all this boring stuff. All these established programs and organizations that appeal to our guilt and sense of duty. We don't realize we can do a hell of a lot more good a hell of a lot more cheaply by supporting stuff that's fun and that people actually *like* instead of these bureaucratic organizations that have all this publicity that are paying someone to work nine to five condescendingly "empowering" people.

A philanthropic artist can fund people to invent their own job descriptions. As an artist of philanthropy, I could fund someone to become an organizer of people who write letters to the editor of newspapers telling their ideas of how to fix the country!

These are people who are crying out for a better world and their letters go ignored. No one goes to ask them, What's stopping you from doing something about this? Are you connected with these and these and these other people who share your concerns? What resources would you need to make this happen? And no one stays in touch with them and encourages them and helps them meet people and strategize their course of action.

There is no job description like that.

An artist of philanthropy could create one.

This is a whole new frontier of philanthropy and community organizing and social activism that hasn't happened yet and that desperately needs to happen if we're going to make it through the next century.

When people think of art, they think of painting, sculpture, music, dance, theater, film and writing. But those are only *media* of art. They are only art *forms*. But if you think of art not as a form but as a spirit—an imaginative force that can take many forms—then money can be used as a medium of art!

The reason it may be hard to see money as a medium of art is that money isn't usually used artistically. Traditionally, money and material resources have been used in an incredibly boring and unoriginal way. When it comes to money, most of us are pretty shitty artists. If we were rated on our use of money the way artists are rated on their artwork, Siskel and Ebert would probably give us all a two-thumbs down except for a few rare people who are ahead of their time. That's okay. As a civilization, we're still in the Dark Ages about philanthropy. It really only became identified as a field in this century with Carnegie, Rockefeller, and Ford, and now it has become professionalized which has set it back hundreds of years. But the great thing about philanthropy is that it doesn't have to be professionalized and killed like the other professions. Wealthy individuals can choose to do philanthropy however the hell they want. Most big foundations insist that their Program Officers have high level degrees. Why? Why do degrees make you better at giving away money?

Most wealthy people are not trying to do anything very interesting with their money. But there are exceptions. And the lucky thing is, it doesn't take very many exceptions to make an enormous impact. I see my job as finding and encouraging other exceptions—other exceptional rich people, young or old—who aren't satisfied with the way philanthropy is done in this country, and who want to experiment with other, more powerful, more imaginative, more enjoyable, ways of doing it. People who see philanthropy as an art form are going to get together and we're going to build a philanthropic arts movement and we're going to *make* philanthropy into the most powerful art form of the 21st Century. How are we going to change the bullshit that passes for philanthropy today? With real philanthropy—the power of love!

THE ART OF PHILANTHROPY

1. You don't have to be rich to be a philanthropist. According to Kim Klein, Editor of Grassroots Fundraising Journal, 82% of individual giving in this country comes from people with incomes under $60,000.

2. Spread love. Someone could give away millions. If they don't love people and treat people well in their personal as well as work life, then their hypocrisy is eventually going to catch up with them and hurt their cause. Some people spread love wherever they go. They deserve to reap what they sow. It's easier to help someone with an extraordinary love to build a viable organization than it is to help a viable organization to spread love. Support people who you think are really good people with a total commitment to doing good in the world and who are willing to put their asses on the line to do it.

3. Originality and imagination. If it makes you laugh out loud or say "Wow!" then support it.

4. Support people who have guts. It's so rare.

5. Support unpopular truths. People who speak truth to power and who speak their truth no matter how unpopular it is.

6. Historical players. Support people who are strategic and thoughtful about their work in the context of history.

7. Out of the loop and under the radar. If you've heard of an organization, chances are they aren't out-of-the loop. Support people who no one else is supporting. Support people who are less likely to have connections or be understood by most people who give away money.

8. Effective and cost-effective. Support people who will stretch your charity dollar as wisely or more wisely than you would stretch it.

9. Fund passions over nine to fives. Support people whose work is their passion in life, not a nine to five job.

10. Self-help not poor little you. Support self-help organizations rather than "let me help you" charities. I believe in every person's and every group's right to self-determination. It's very simple, I know. But most charities are anti-self-determination. They are based on the top-down "poor little you"model.

I'm suggesting organizations led by people who come from or are still a part of the class of people they are helping. So if the organization works with "at-risk youth" I want to know that the leadership of the organization is mainly people who either are or used to be "at-risk youth."

11. Root causes, not Band-Aids. Self-help isn't enough. The whole system needs to be changed. The groups that have the hardest time getting money are the ones fighting to change the system. Yet less than 1% of all charitable giving goes to social change. The slogan of the social change philanthropy movement is, "Change, not charity." Amen! That's where your money will go the farthest.

12. Doers not grantwriters. I like people who are more interested in doing their work than in raising money from me. I like to support people who are *not* good fundraisers. And then I give them a copy of Kim Klein's incredible fundraising video, available from the Headwaters Fund in Minneapolis. Let the good fundraisers get someone else's money.

13. "Visionaries who can implement." I stole this phrase from a ingenious little foundation called Ashoka: Innovators for the Public. The visionary who can implement is a rare combination.

14. Combinationism and collaboration. Support people who combine fields—they aren't just into art, they aren't just into politics, they aren't just into science, but instead they combine many fields. Support organizations that bring together and value very different kinds of people rather than organizations which bring together relatively homogenous groups.

15. Glue people, not narrow geniuses. Support people who lead integrated lives, whose closest friends and allies cross the boundaries of class and race and who uphold the utmost personal integrity in their lives.

16. Net gains. Funding an ex-con to become a community organizer is a bigger net gain for society than funding someone with a college degree. The college student can get another good job. The ex-con probably can't.

17. Pay general operating expenses. If you really believe in an organization, help them buy a building so they can become sustainable and quit paying rent to a landlord. Don't dictate how they should spend the money.

18. Trust what inspires you.

CONCLUSIONS

NO MORE PRISONS
MORE OF EVERYTHING ELSE

I am aware that at first glance No More Prisons may not seem like the world's most creative or appropriate title for this book.

That's because most of the creativity is in the *structure* and the *economics* of the title, more than in its face-value meaning. I chose the title first and foremost because I wanted to support two young activists, Rishi Nath and Vincent

Merry, from Raptivism Records, who are putting out a benefit hip-hop compilation album with the same name. The creativity is in the partnership between a hip-hop record label and a punk rock book publisher, Soft Skull Press.

The book and the album have nothing to do with each other, except for the name. My strategy was to market them together, hit both audiences, and confuse the shit out of everyone. Raptivism's audience will be tempted into buying a book. My audience will be hoodwinked into buying a hip-hop album. And we'll both be able to raise more money for the causes we believe in.

Like fighting the prison industry.

"Okay, picture this. I was teaching a GED math class in Chicago," says Rishi. "I'm trying to teach my class. The police come and arrest one of my students. They pull him right out of class—for missing a court date. Then I went to visit another one of my students who's in a maximum security prison for three years on petty charges, having a sexual relationship with an underaged girl. It was a mutual relationship, but she was a ward of the state so he got prosecuted for statutory rape. Now his cellmate is a murderer. You got teachers with no health benefits teaching GED and you got cops and prison guards with much health benefits getting paid to lock up kids for petty offenses. Then I'm walking home from school. I keep getting stopped. Who was I? Why was I there? Why was I on 52nd and Drexel at night? I was like, 'I'm a teacher and I live on this block.' They had the whole street cordoned off. They were like, 'We don't care. Where's your ID?' I was like, 'Wait a minute.' We're trying to educate students. You're trying to lock them up. That's when it clicked for me. That's when all the prison statistics started making sense. That's when I realized it's not enough to work with one kid at a time. It's not enough for me to do education and hip-hop. I had to become a prison activist."

At first, seeing himself as an activist wasn't a natural thing for Rishi.

"There's no such thing as a hip-hop activist movement, so we had to make it up. At first I was turned off by activism because it was bureaucratic. The issues were good, but could I stomach the dryness? We had to learn from all these people who can sustain organizations—like Kevin Pranis at Democratic Socialists of America (DSA), Africa Porter at Operation PUSH, and others who aren't hip-hop artists, but who are feeling it and who are invested in us. When I would go back to my hip-hop community, people would know what time it was, but there was no structure. I realized I needed to learn that structure, so I just had to stomach it. I learned how to plan conferences, set agendas, all the stuff that was boring to me a few years ago, but I learned that's how you build an organization."

Rishi got together with his friend Vincent Merry. The organization they built was Raptivism Records. Their first project is the *No More Prisons* CD featuring: Group Home, The Anomalies, Daddy-O, Lil' Dap from OGC,

Apani, Rubberoom, Hurricane G, Dead Prez, Cornel West, Chubb Rock, Danny Hoch, The Last Poets, Akbar, Cocoa Brovaz, Edo G, Boots from The Coup, L Da Head Toucha, who all donated tracks.

Vincent Merry quit Howard Medical School to become an activist. He now works for the Urban Justice Center in New York. "As a doctor, you treat one patient at a time once they're already sick. And I realized what I'm really interested in is innovation and solutions to society's deeper problems. I saw a lot of people who were interested in becoming doctors. I didn't see a lot of people who were committed to sweeping social change. Not just saying, 'Cops are fucked up. Too many of my peoples are locked up. That's messed up,' But taking that voice, that frustration, that energy, and channeling it into a real movement.

"We're calling on the hip-hop audience to say, 'We're not having this anymore.' We're gonna use our voice to put together money that will finance a movement to stop the expansion of the prison system. We're saying that if even a fraction of the money that's spent on prisons was reinvested in the community, we could deal with these problems in a better way. That's what *No More Prisons* is all about."

There is a growing grassroots movement in this country to halt the expansion of the prison system the same way the generation before us worldwide stopped the war in Vietnam. Like with Vietnam, we are up against a war machine, and a media stream of myths based on fear. Our movement doesn't have much money and it is not very well organized yet. So our cause isn't going to be very popular at first, but as more and more people learn what is going on, and as more middle-class parents find out little Johnny and Jennifer are doing five-year mandatory minimums for having two hits of acid, the tide is going to change. The opposition is going to grow.

I was made aware of the prison problem because my best friend Gita Drury helped organize Critical Resistance, the first major across-the-board mega-conference for prison activists. Gita had done an internship with Legal Services for Prisoners with Children (LSPC) in San Francisco. They file class-action lawsuits on behalf of women inmates. When Gita was there, LSPC was working on a class-action lawsuit for medical neglect:

"I was interviewing women prisoners in central California in a town called Chowchilla, which has two women's prisons right across the street from one another," Gita recalls. "They hold over 2500 inmates—each! And I was just awestruck to meet all these women many of whom's crime was merely being at the wrong place at the wrong time. And what initially inspired me was thinking about how it very easily could have been me if things had been different in my life and so I said, 'Why should I not care about what goes on behind prison walls just because none of my friends or family happen to be there? Or just because most of the people who are in power in this country don't have a family member who's locked up? And that just has to do with demographics and who's in power and who's not. Some of the women have done pretty horrific things. Most of them haven't. I interviewed one woman who stole a vacuum cleaner, and she got seven years because of prior offenses. And she has AIDS dementia which means she's mentally unstable much of the time. This woman is dying in prison because she stole a vacuum cleaner!"

The stories Gita told me convinced me that if there is one evil force at a state and national level that can unite Americans of different races and classes, across sex, religion and sexual orientation, it's the expansion of the prison industry.

Last year, I read about the case of Shareef Cousin who was convicted of shooting a white man in the head in New Orleans' French Quarter. He was sentenced to the death at age 16. Not only was Shareef innocent of the murder (he was at a basketball game), there was *video footage he was playing basketball at the time of the killing.*

I was passing through New Orleans, a retired graffiti writer. I read about Shareef's case. It made me so angry that it brought me out of retirement. In six hours I painted hundreds of sidewalks in the French Quarter and downtown New Orleans: "Shareef may be innocent." "Shareef deserves a fair trial." "Please don't kill Shareef."

I wrote on sidewalks only, not on walls. The goal was to make a moral claim on the conscience of the city, not to alienate anyone who could become a juror in Shareef's new trial. Graffiti requires a higher standard of responsibility when you're dealing with someone's life.

Three days before the retrial was set to begin, the District Attorney inexplicably dropped the murder charges. Shareef Cousin was taken off of death row.

Did graffiti influence the DA's decision to free Shareef Cousin?

We can never know. What matters is that it helped create a climate of unacceptability toward murdering him in our name. But more importantly, word got out in the graffiti world and it woke graffiti writers up to the power of connecting our work to concrete social movements.

Now hundreds of us—graffiti writers and concerned citizens alike—are taking up spray paint and writing, "No More Prisons" on sidewalks of busy intersections and shopping mall parking lots across America—the first ever large-scale graffiti civil disobedience campaign. I am not the leader of it and I cannot speak for anyone else, but I am willing to face any legal retribution I may encounter for expressing my beliefs in this way. Building more prisons at this point in American history is immoral and self-destructive to our social fabric. Painting on the sidewalk is an act of free speech which doesn't hurt anyone and doesn't even "damage" the sidewalk (the paint rubs off in a few months.) The social and spiritual damage we are doing by building more prisons and filling them with non-violent offenders will haunt us for generations to come.

The hip-hop nation has never before successfully attached itself to a political movement. The Million Man March was not a movement against a system, it was a self-help rally. The Stop The Violence "Movement" of the 1980s was not a movement. It was a slogan and a song benefit with the backwards idea to raise money for the Urban League, a mild-mannered organization of aging civil rights leaders. It should have been the other way around. The civil rights generation should be raising money to support the political leaders of the hip-hop generation. That's part of why our generation has no recognizable political leaders—we have no major organizations that support them. The prison movement represents the most immediate reason in a generation for young people to get involved with political organizing.

Two other things impress me about prison activism: 1) The prison industry is so bad that, like segregation in the South during the 1950s and '60s, it forces people to unite who would ordinarily refuse to work together. 2) How rapidly learning about prisons blows the minds of sheltered white people.

My old roommate in D.C., Daniel Burton-Rose, is from a small town in Ohio. Been around white people his whole life. In college he got involved with Oberlin Action Against Prisons, one of the first and best prison activist groups on a college campus. He wasn't an activist or a published writer. But there was such a gap in information about the prison system that by the time Daniel was 19 years old, he edited *The Celling of America* (Common Courage Press, 1998), an anthology of political essays by prisoners. I asked Daniel what he thought was the best way for college kids to fight the prison industry.

"The most radical thing for college kids is talking to prisoners and getting to know them," Daniel says. "When I was 18, I was living in a small town in Colorado and I was corresponding with prisoners in some of the most abusive, mind-deadening prisons in the world. The great thing about people having prison activism as their first activist experience, as opposed to tutoring kids or saving the whales or something, is that you get to see directly how the government really treats people. You get to see how the government lies. You get to see how hideous and destructive those correctional facilities are. I interviewed this one woman who was in jail for petty theft. They put her in a private prison, and while she was in there she got raped by a prison guard. She organized a posse of women in prison who have been sexually abused by guards and they're starting to make some noise. Prison activism sucked in and radicalized all these people at Oberlin who I never expected to become activists— I never even thought of them as political entities. From time to time, I'd check on the group and ask, 'Who's in the prison group now?' And then they'd tell me and I'd say, 'No! That person? I can't believe it!'"

I ask Daniel, *"If people wanted to start a prison group on a campus, would you know what to tell them?"*

"Yeah. This woman called me the other day from Brown University. She's starting a prison group there and I knew exactly what to tell her. You get a bunch of films so you can do self-education as well as educating the campus. Then you get permission to go into a local prison in your area. I was like, 'Look in the medical wing. Look at what the prison's isolation policies are. Look at whether they shackle women when they give birth. If they take their babies away from them. Look at prison labor. How much are they getting paid? And for what? Is it dangerous to their health? I know of cases where prisoners have been made to pull asbestos out of walls with their bare hands. How much are they paying them? How much are they charging families of prisoners to receive phone calls . . . ' All these questions my friend who was a political prisoner, Bo Brown, told me to have people ask."

On a more personal level, I'm finding myself in a position where I actually have the opportunity of selling out. I have an agent. He tried to sell *Bomb the Suburbs* to a major publisher. The editors liked it. It went all the way up to Mr. Head of Books at the Evil Stepparent Company, Time Warner. Mr. Head, I am told, lives in the suburbs and he usually rubber-stamps all book projects, but it seems he made a special exception for me.

My agent was disappointed but he reassured me, "Don't worry. You sold 23,000 copies on your own. I'm sure someone will want it."

I was like good. I could use a nice, fat book advance.

Then I could start two organizations and buy a house and have a whole rack of other young activists living with me. And together we could rock this planet and turn the party out. And I wouldn't have to do all the boring work of distributing and publicizing and arranging my own book tour. I'd be free to actually write and talk about the ideas in my book.

And maybe I'd even have time to read other books, and play sports, see my friends, experience sunlight, and detach myself from this evil computer screen.

But then I start thinking about what these big publishers are really going to do with my book. I won't control the cover art. If someone called me and wanted to reprint a chapter, I couldn't just say, "Sure." I'd have to say, "Fax a letter to the Legal Department." All the independent bookstores and distributors who supported the book would now have to pay *more* for it than Borders or Barnes & Noble. All the kids who had a part in creating it, who put up posters, who sold it at their schools and on public transit and who read it over and over and passed it to their friends wouldn't feel the same sense of ownership and pride anymore. I wouldn't be able to let people order 10 and 20 copies for $4.50 each. Instead it would cost them $14.95. I couldn't give away free copies to people who picked me up hitchhiking. I couldn't get a printer that uses union labor or recycled paper. And I wouldn't even own the rights to my own book. If the publisher let it go out of print then it would just be gone. This book is too important to me to put in the hands of a multinational corporation.

I decided to self-publish.

With a twist.

A twist by the name of Sander Hicks. Sander Hicks has a band called White Collar Crime, but he has a blue collar job. He is a superintendent of an apartment building on Manhattan's Lower East Side, and he runs Soft Skull Press out of the basement. He has published 42 books so far, written five plays, and he's down with every cause on the Lower East Side, from urban gardens, to fighting gentrification, to squatters, to police harassment.

And he's only 28 years old.

So watch out.

We are splitting the profits. Soft Skull's half of the profits will help Sander grow the Press, which he doesn't make any money off of. My half will go to support The Active Element Foundation, which funds youth activists who are fighting for the values we talk about in here.*

So thank you for buying this book!

It costs you $12. The store gets about $5 of that. The distributor gets another $1.50. Our cost per book is about $3, including overhead. So that leaves $2.50 per book in profit. Half of that goes to Soft Skull, and the other half goes to support the Active Element Foundation. If it sells as many copies as *Bomb the Suburbs,* it will raise $30,000 for Active Element, which is enough to hire two part-time staff for a year. That will allow them to raise many times that to fund young activists who are doing everything they can to fight for a better tomorrow.

On behalf of everyone involved, I thank you for investing in your future and ours.

I'm serious about my craft as an artist and I'm serious about living my beliefs. As important to me as anything written in this book is the fact that it is printed on recycled paper at United Graphics, an employee-owned company in Mattoon, Illinois. They are located down in South Central Illinois, "The Zone" where Catepillar and Staley workers recently waged a long battle against downsizing.

One of the ideas in this book is to expand our understanding of what is art. We always think of art as painting, writing, dance, film or music. Later for that. Later for brilliant but narrow artists who don't know how to treat their friends or raise their kids or take care of business.

---

* The Active Element Foundation was created to inspire a new generation of philanthropists to fund courageous young activists who aren't supported by traditional foundations. Afrika Bambaataa identified the original four elements of hip-hop in the early '70s: MCing (rap), b-boying (dance), writing (graffiti), and DJing. But at the same time Bambaataa started the Zulu Nation, which was a youth organization. From the very beginning, The Active Element has been the foundation of hip-hop.

I want to talk about the art of being human and having relationships. Isn't it a creative act to cooperate across race and class? Isn't it an art to figure out how to live your values in a fucked-up society without going crazy? I don't hear a lot about the art of building organizations and movements that will keep us from ending life on Earth. Why isn't that considered art? The art of living is a constant art, a multi-dimensional art. It's an art you can't capture in a book or a CD or even on the side of a train. That's because human relationships are the hardest art, and the most neglected. Ultimately it is my respect for Raptivism's work and the work of so many who are fighting the prison system that made me name this book *No More Prisons*.

THE ORGANIZATIONS WE NEED

Writing a book doesn't change shit. Neither does writing graffiti. To change history, you need to build organizations. Organizations channel the energies of people who want things to change. That's why we need new organizations in each of these five areas: The prison-industrial complex; Urban life versus suburban sprawl; self-education and homeschooling; hip-hop and urban leadership; cool rich kids and philanthropy.

And we need all five to work together.

Why do we need all five?

Because each by itself has a fatal flaw.

The Prison Industry

The anti-prison movement is promising, but it needs all the allies it can get. We need educators and others who have experienced the brunt of the budget cuts over the past 20 years to wake the fuck up and flex their political muscle. We need a South Africa-style disinvestment campaign by churches and universities and socially responsible investors to rid their portfolios of Wackenhut, Corrections Corporation of America, Cornell, and other publicly-traded companies which are profiting from prison construction. And you can't have a movement without rich and white people because you'll have no resources to sustain it and the power structure will clobber you, and you'll still be poor at the end of the day. Prisoners who are educating themselves need connections to the broader self-education movement. And they desperately need the political leadership of those in the hip-hop generation who aren't locked up yet to step forward and organize.

Neighborhood Life vs. Suburban Sprawl

The movement for a vital urban life, public life and community life is promising, but it's run by old white guys. It needs life! It needs hip-hop! And it's too hard to have a movement when young people are being taught to hate public life in pre-prison-like places called public schools. And you can't build a movement for a vital public and civic life unless foundation and nonprofit people are willing to commit major resources to funding and supporting the tens of thousands of tiny grassroots groups which make public life thrive. We need organizations of artists and hip-hop activists and punk-rock kids and small business owners and older people (who've been around long enough to remember what real neighborhoods are like) to join forces in protecting what's left of urban public life.

Self-Education and Homeschooling

The self-education movement doesn't exist yet. The homeschooling movement is promising but it's too white and too segregated and too isolated from public life and there's not enough infrastructure to support poor people who want to educate themselves, let alone prisoners. It needs hip-hop leadership! We need an all-ages, multi-racial self-education movement that re-energizes public life and is supported by a generation of self-education foundations and self-education resource centers that allow more young people and families to do it.

Hip-Hop and Urban Leadership

The emerging hip-hop leadership is promising but they have a lot to learn from rich and white people about how to move a political agenda and build institutions in this society. And they aren't getting enough support from cool rich and white people. And shitty schools and neighborhoods and prisons are destroying their families. And when public life is dead—when streets are abandoned, and buses don't run, and libraries close early, then how are you going to become a community leader? And most of the foundations, nonprofits, activists and organizers who are supposed to be nurturing these young leaders are completely out-of-touch. We need organizations and foundations that recognize and support young urban leaders on their own terms. And we need a new generation of urban kids to become scholars and community organizers and entrepreneurs, not just rappers and graffiti writers.

Cool Rich Kids

A cool rich kids movement barely exists. Rich folks have a lot to learn from poor people about resourcefulness. But they're not gonna live in mixed neighborhoods if there's no vibrant public life and if they have to send their kids to shitty public schools. And they aren't going to support grassroots organizations unless they have personal connections with the people who run them.

And they're not going to join mixed-income, mixed-race communities unless there's a movement to build these communities. And that requires the support of foundations, nonprofits, community organizers and activists. We need a new generation of cool rich folks to fund the creation of hyper-grassroots foundations that can understand, identify and support the real grassroots leaders in every community, the "out-of-pocket sector" who do the work of the not-for-profit sector out of their own empty pockets when the paid do-gooders go home—and who have the freedom and independence to challenge government and corporations doing wrong. And the vision to fund the invention of new organizations such as the ones discussed below:

Are you seeing now how all the themes in this book connect? How we need new organizations in each of these five areas, and how they all need each other?

WHY YOU NEED TO START YOUR OWN ORGANIZATION

When I say we need new organizations in each of these five areas, I don't just mean we need two or three organizations. I mean we need thousands and thousands of organizations all over the world with different angles and different bases of support.

Why don't you start one?

Yes.

You personally.

Stop playing shy.

I know you want to start an organization.

If you didn't, you wouldn't have made it this far in the book.

A lot of people don't like organizations. People think they're boring and ineffective and they suck the life out of whatever good cause they're supposedly working for. My response, "Good, then you start one. We need someone like you to start an organization that will cut through the bullshit and change things for real."

A lot of people who are already in organizations say, "We don't need any more organizations. There are enough organizations. Why not support the ones we already have?"

The problem is not that we have too many organizations. The problem is we have too many disconnected, disappointing, turf-squabbling organizations, and not enough organizations that people really like. There are a lot of organizations that I like. I spend a lot of time learning about them and trying to support them any way I can.

But for every organization I like, there are a thousand gaps where an organization needs to be where one isn't.

In Albuquerque, New Mexico, there is a great organization called Youth Action which supports and networks youth-led activist groups around the country. They are an incredible group. The problem is they are only able to support a few dozen organizations. Are they winning significant local victories? Yes. On a national scale are they even making a dent? Hardly. To make a serious dent, we need tens of thousands more activist organizations. And eventually we need them to be networked and coordinated.

But that comes later.

First we need them to simply exist.

Then we can network them.

But why not just have one big organization, you ask?

Here's why.

There isn't the support to create one big organization until you have hundreds and thousands of micro-organizations.

A perfect example of how this works is with NOA, the National Organizer's Alliance. NOA is an organization of 2000 community organizers from around the country. The members of NOA represent all different organizations, many of which could never even begin to agree with each other. That's fine. We don't have to. NOA provides space for us to come together and talk. It sends us a newsletter that lists job openings. It's funny. It holds conferences which are fun. You can get health insurance through them. NOA is run with integrity and spirit. It makes community organizers feel appreciated and connected and welcome.

And then it gets out of our way.

Should NOA try to become a big organization which swallows its members and makes us all sit in a room and agree on one thing?

Hell, no.

It's great the way it is.

We need something like NOA for micro-organizations.

Yet another organization that the art of philanthropy needs to create!

THE JOY OF ORGANIZING

I'm not dissing big organizations. If someone wanted to create a big organization tomorrow I'd be down to help them.

But there's a reason why someone like me would be down to help. It's *because I've had the personal experience* of starting my own organization. People learn by doing. People only truly care about something they have intimate personal experience with. People who've waited tables give better tips.

There is a developmental process to movement-building and it starts with small groups experimenting with building organizations and engaging the people around them. Before you start a big organization, you need a critical mass of people who feel personally connected to the struggle and belong to a group they have faith in. An organization like Greenpeace or the NAACP is simply too big to make most of its members feel personally connected.

Don't get me wrong. We need big organizations. But we also need tens of millions of one person and two person and three person micro-organizations which connect to and energize and challenge the bigger ones. Information technology and organizational development workshops are making it easier for people to start their own little groups. The emerging revolution in philanthropy is beginning to make it easier for small, innovative groups to get money.

And no, it doesn't just mean more groups are going to be competing for the same dollar. Philanthropy is not a zero-sum game. By starting more organizations that people *like,* we can expand the philanthropic pie. The more people start organizations, and the more people get their friends and family involved, the more we can expand the pie.

Example: I got my parents to contribute $1000 to *No More Prisons.* They've never made a $1000 gift before. That money will go to publicize this book which will raise money for the Active Element Foundation which will fund tons of small youth activist groups my parents have never even heard of. But because of their personal connection to me, they will begin to hear about them, and care about them. Then they will be more likely to give them money.

I want you to think seriously about starting an organization. It doesn't have to be a big organization. It could just be you. Think about your skills, resources, connections, *passions* and dream up a way to fight evil in your own little personal and specific way. Make up a clever name for it. Then call your friends. Get them excited about it. If they're not excited, then make some new friends who are. Have them over for dinner. Make it fun.

And don't spend too much time planning. The most important step is to start the organization. Learn by doing. It will probably flop and that's okay. It's your first try. You'll learn as you go. I have probably started a dozen organizations that flopped. That's okay. I had to fail to learn. I had to fail to meet the people who would eventually help me succeed. I had to fail to understand what my weaknesses were and what I was really trying to build. I am still trying to figure it out. I am writing this essay from scratch on the last day before this book is due at the printer.

People who run existing organizations may feel threatened by all this talk about people starting their own organizations. The turf issue. Folks need to check themselves with that turf shit. Folks need to ask themselves why they're really doing this work in the first place. Everyone doing social change work says their goal is to fix the problems and work themselves out of a job. But when the next generation of people you've been working to "empower" comes along and starts to crowd your section of the movement, are you really down to pass the torch?

At the same time, people who are starting new organizations need to appreciate their elders, instead of tearing their elders down to elevate themselves. You're gonna be an elder some day too, if you're lucky. And the youngsters who come along after you are gonna think *your* shit is tired. Everyone needs to appreciate the people before them. I can sit up here and dis foundations and schools and hip-hop all day, but I'll be damned if I don't appreciate all the incredible and pathbreaking people who've moved these fields over the past 30 years. I have mad respect for my elders, and pioneers and everyone who contributed to the movements that birthed me. I study their work. I call them up. I ask questions. I send them people. I send them money. I send them love.

The organizational start-up revolution is going to shake-up the activist world the same way Internet start-ups are shaking up corporate America. Organizations that can adapt to working with a rack of young upstarts will flourish. Organizations that believe they are the center of the universe will lose relevance.

It is difficult to grasp this moment in the history of life on Earth. Those of us who get it some of the time—who appreciate the sanctity, and who understand our power in determining the future—we have a lot of work to do. There are billions of things we must do to continue to preserve life on Earth. There are billions of strategies. Billions of people must realize what our special roles are in protecting life on Earth.

This isn't just about an issue for me. It isn't just about justice or peace or freedom or equality. It's about our very survival. The challenge before us as a human race in ensuring our own continuation is the most difficult challenge that has ever faced anyone in the history of life on Earth.

Want a challenge?

Because all of the people who helped me and kept me sane.

THE REASON WHY I'M NOT IN PRISON

Barbara, Bill, and Nonny who went through hell raising me.
You're my favorite prison wardens of all!

My second family, the Chicago hip-hop community who I left to do this.
I love y'all. I want to take you with me. Here, I brought you back something.
This book.

To Lisa Sullivan and the crew at LISTEN Inc.
Ditra Edwards, Teresa Sule, Makuti Lee, Catilla Everette, Rehva Scotman,
Raquel Gutierrez, and Kenneth Bailey. You have all taught me so much. I'm
proud to be part of the team!

Raptivism, Soft Skull, Active Element, and Self-Education Foundation:
Rishi Nath, Vin Merry, Sander Hicks and crew (Cat Tyc, Susan Mitchell,
Adam Young, Amier Carmel), Danny Hoch, J-Love (Jennifer Calderon), Kofi
Taha, Gita Drury, Emily Nepon, Karl T. Muth, and Adriyel Paymer. We are
building this together!

The dopest woman on the planet, Gita Jai Drury.
I love you. You more than anyone else supported me in this.

**People who contributed to the creation of No More Prisons and put them-
selves on the line to help me**
Kat Aaron, Seshat Yohimbe aka Lutisha Phillips, Pete Miser, Kevin Powell,
Christine Wong, Martin Sprause, John Payne, Vivien Labaton, Molly Hein,
Lisa Sullivan, Easter Maynard, Josh MacPhee, Kim Gaines, Adam Mansbach
(and your books Shackling Water and Laugh/Riot), Adam Stenftenagel,
Rahmaan Barnes, Steven Feuerstein, Chris and Viva Silva, Micah Bazant, Sofia
Quintero, Ditra Edwards, Rachel Dobkin, Brian Sleet, Reggie Dennis and the
folks at Manifest, David Jacobs, Donna Frisby, Angela Wheeler, Anne Slepian
and Christopher Mogil, Daniel Burton-Rose, Salim Muwakkil, Gita Drury,
Riccardo Cortes, Mike Lapham, Jim, Joan, Danielle and Jacob Shapiro, Erica
Thornton, Allen Gordon, Anne and Eben Carlson, Stan Hallett, Marc Spiegler,
Seeta Ganghadaran, Marta Drury.

Friends, mentors, allies and touchstones in this work
Liza Featherstone, Jay Imani and Third Eye Movement, Underground Railroad, Olin, Robin Templeton, Julie Brown, Jeff Chang and Colorlines, Toni Blackman, Windy Chien, Dru, Carmen Mitchell, kwami the Qster, Strath, Ben Ortiz, Abdul Alkalimat, Neal Pollack, Danny Postel, Kari Lydersen, Mark Armstrong, Rachel Timoner, David Hale Smith, Neri Holguin, Eli Lee, John Peck, Anton, Angela Wheeler, Grace Llewellyn, April Rosenblum, James Bernard, Rob Marriott, Michelle Gaza, Teal, C3PO, and the MUL crew, Randy Ingstrom, Mear, Connie Julian, Megan Jones, Suchi Swift, Alix Spiegel, Ira Glass, Dulce, One-9, dream hampton, Sasha Altman DuBrul, Rusty Stahl and Jamal Watson, Pat Arden, Alison True, Jay Readey, Jeremy Relph, Dalton Higgins, Judith Helfand, Nikki Stewart, Rafael, Jamie Schweizer, Barre-Lynn Tapia, Roberto Sanchez, Steven Donziger, Wendy Day, Kalle Lasn, Amanda Huron, Mary Jane and Mike Yurchak, Gabriel and Hector Calderon, Luis Cardona, Adam Gold, Lely Constantinople, Scoop, Chris Leatzow, Leslie Thomas, Alain "Ket" Mariduena, Vee Bravo, Clyde Valentine and the crew at Stress Magazine, Tracy Gary, Lloyd King, Vicky, Youth Struggling for Survival, Pat Zamora, Micheal Warr, Luis Rodriguez, Karuna Scheinfeld, Eddie Ellis, Hector Torres, Raybblin Vargas (I respect your important contribution even if we disagree.), Jon Caramanica, Akilah Watkins, Walda Katz-Fishman from Project South, Ian from Open Voice, Boots, David Prince, Lisa and Deb Stulberg, Jeremy Davis, Jacob Snyder, David Sepkowski, Allen Hancock, Wali, Josh Glenn, Carol and Katie Pencke, Bill Capowski, B-Boy B, Warp, Cashus D, Ben Hall, Mik and Deborah, Cassandra Shaylor, Cindy Chandler, Terry Miller, Megan Jasper, Anne, Eben, Shoes and Bert Carlson, Heath Row, Michael Hsu, Aaron Edison, Rosanna Orfield, Carol and Katie Pencke, Si Kahn, Samantha Stainburn, Ben Kim, Leslie Crutchfield, Ben Higa, Anthony Qaiyum, Heather Booth, Megan Jones, Ta-Nehisi Coates, Riz Rollins, Rhyme Fest, Benia andSolomon, Ang 13, Erin Potts, Jon Voss, Allen Gordon, Paul Resnick, Van Jones, Amy Richards, Namane Mohlambane, Marta, Pedro, and Marian Urquilla, Easter Maynard & Matt Rebello, Angela Davis, Ellen Barry, Ruthie Gilmore, Pam Mitchell (In the Basement), The Klonsky family, The Heinemann-Piepers, Mario, Tina Howell, Kendall Lloyd, Tara Betts, Monica Menduno, Kevin and Jenny Luklan, Reggie Royston, Dre, Los, Most Dangerous, Bessie, Spirit, Chris, Laz, Corie, Kelt, SMK, and everyone from the Hip-hop Federation, The Movement Foundation, Brad Ott, Tracy Hoare, Naomi Swinton, Matt Stephens, Aceyalone, Ahmir Hampton, Victor and Aya, Barbara Meyer, Jamal Reid, Dream Nefra, Mark Reed, Daris Illunga, Melissa Bradley, Naomi Swinton, Melissa Kohner, Mike Vasquez, Lindsay Waters, Cornel West, Juliette Randolph, Priscilla Mendizabal, Charles Lamar, Lashika Hopper, Claudia Melgar, Wayan Vota, Lew Rosenbaum, Eric Utne, John Spayde, Malika Saada Saar, Craig Harshaw, Ayanna Salusbury, Nunya Pongo, Dzine, Lee

Ballinger from Rock and Rap Confidential, Catherine Gund, Melanie Hope, Brett Webb, Amanda Cooper, Maurci Jackson, Espo, Ari, Siobhan Reynolds, Pugsly Adams, Amanda Klonsky, EC Illa, Mickey, Sinbad and the Wicked crew, Legendary Traxster and the CWAL crew, Eskae and Sundance, Dream and Spie, Mike Lapham, Farah Grey, Rinku Sen, Mark Breimhorst, Bergen O'Mally, Caroline Durham, Gary Delgado, Danielle Gecko, Brendan Dooley, Conee Rock, Marco Davis, Jackie Velez, Nicole Johnson, Natalie Avery, The Kensington Welfare Rights Union, Cheri Honkala, Marc Weber, Mattie, Jessica Alvarez, Alyssa Scheunemann, Dana Gilette, Isaac Hodes, Terry Marshall, Kristin Brown, jessica Care moore,Wyatt Mitchell, Hunter Brumfield, Ben Higa, Drew, Rhea Vedro, Gnee, Calvin Baker, Alison Byrne-Fields, Terry and Sam Evans, Wes Jackson, Jessica Tully, Andrew Boyd, Jay Walljasper, Ben Smilowitz, Jen Baumgarder, Nomy Lamm, Mary Margaret, Media Island, Nikki Morse, Jeremy Davis, Jordan Howland, Common, Sano, Lavie and Risha Raven, Manju, Billy, Ruby Love, My family: Jay and Caroline, Ben, Marguerite and Bill Horberg, Sarajo Frieden, Miro Horberg-Frieden, Ruth, Jeff and the twins, John John, John and Kathy, Mary and Shelley, Mike and Ted, Jeff and Kim, Hot House, Paul Bass, Karuna Scheinfeld, Liz Lazdins-Pinkham, Tim Rogers, Kevin McAlester, Kestrel and Elijah, Kamau Marcharia, Eboo Patel from the Interfaith Youth Corps, Elena White-Negrete, Eric, Breeze Lutke-Stahlman, Anthony Qaiyum, Malaika Sanders and LaTonya, Angela Brown, Zenobia Spencer, Shae Lim, Jade Crown, Dorsey Nunn, Anna, Ian, and the Fritz family, Africa Porter, Thomas Goldstein, Aaron Edison, Charles Aaron, Kiese Laymon, Nico Berry, Sandra Manthe, Gesa and Glenn, Amy Weinberg, Francoisie, Taj James, Sea, Javier, Chris Golden, Masami, Jesse De le Pena, Reginald Jolley, Paul Teruel, Matt Schwartz, Chang Lin, Stoop, Kareem Hasan, Iggy Scam, Sami and Arianna, Jomo, Mumia Abu-Jamal, Noel Ignatiev, Heidi Scheussler, Raymond O'Neal, Wayan Vota, Mos Def and Talib Kweli, April Silver, Yvonne Bynoe, Kim Davis, DavidScheingold, Amy Quinn, Nicole Gudzowski, Patrick Meehan, Jackie McCarthy, Wendy Lesko, Turaj Zaimi, Ann Caton, KSO, Ericka Taylor and Bineshi Albert from Youth Action, Rev. Eugene Rivers III, Yvonne Bynoe, Nick Honore and the Humble Quest, Dead Prez, Magda Rodriguez, Opuriche Miller, Zore, Rhea Vedro, Sam Mulberry, Jamie Kalvin, Sharon Thornton, Ken Dunn, Judith Duncan and Jason, Greg Lucero, John Davis, Jeremy Lahoud, Chloe Eudaly, Ken Dunn, Tiiu McGuire, Master P, Steve Hawkins, Timothea Howard, Kim Fellner, Kelly, Michelle and Robert, Caitlin Palm, Amy Rosenblum, Bob Heuer, Mary Margaret, Noah Prince, Bill Boisvert, John Wilson, Danielle Meltzer and Pete Cassel, John Davis and FAB. AK Press, Marginal, Bookpeople, Koen, Left Bank, Tower, Last Gasp, all the independent distributors and bookstores who supported me when I didn't know what the hell I was doing. Everyone who picked me up by the side of the road. All the people locked up who shouldn't be. And their families.

INDEX

Index

An award-winning reporter, essayist and trend-spotter, William Upski Wimsatt has written for The Chicago Tribune, Vibe, and dozens of other periodicals. His first book, Bomb the Suburbs was a finalist in the Firecracker Alternative Book Awards and sold more than 23,000 copies to date. Upski has spoken at Harvard and Yale and many other colleges although he is a college drop-out.

A former consultant to Rock the Vote on Youth Activism, Upski serves as national talent scout for LISTEN Inc. (The Local Initiative Support Training and Education Network) in Washington DC. He sits on the boards of More than Money, The Active Element Foundation, and the Self Education Foundation. He is co-director with Easter Maynard of Reciprocity, a new organization which brings people together across cultures and disciplines to collaborate on solutions to our common problems.

PHOTO COURTESY OF KIMBERLY C. GAINES

Printed in the United States
by Baker & Taylor Publisher Services